STAR PITCHERS of the Major Leagues

In this book Bill Libby tells the stories of nine outstanding major-league pitchers—how they overcame difficulties, developed their talents and skills, and finally helped lead their teams to victory. The players included are TOM SEAVER, JUAN MARICHAL, DENNIS MC LAIN, JIM MALONEY, DON DRYSDALE, JIM BUNNING, HOYT WILHELM, SAM MC DOWELL *and* BOB GIBSON.

LONGINES
PHILA
12 CF
22 1B
6 RF
15 3B
7 SS
8 2B
16 LF
9 C
14 P
PL 16 12 1B
2B 13 2 3B
AMERICAN
INN R P IG
3 NY 1 1
CHI 0 8
WAS
KC
4 BOS 0 11
BAL 2 1
2 DET 3 10
MIN 0 10
CLE
LA
TUE. NIGHT
PGH. 8 PM
OUT 2
R H E IG
6 8 0
0 0 0
Herald Tribune
Who says a good newspaper has to be dull?

STAR PITCHERS of the Major Leagues

by Bill Libby

Illustrated with photographs

RANDOM HOUSE · NEW YORK

Photograph Credits: Camera 5: Ken Regan ii, 6–7, 30, 72, 128, Lester Sloan 42–43; Malcolm Emmons: vi, 119; Fred Roe: 27 both; United Press International: front and back endpapers, 10, 18, 21, 46, 52, 55, 58, 62, 80, 86, 90, 95, 105, 123, 136; Wide World Photos: 14, 35, 68, 76, 100, 110 both.
Cover: Marvin E. Newman from Multi-Media Photography

This title was originally catalogued by the Library of Congress as follows:

Libby, Bill.
Star pitchers of the major leagues. New York, Random House [1971]

ix, 142 p. illus., ports. 22 cm. (Major league library, 15) $1.95

SUMMARY: Brief biographical sketches of nine major league pitchers: Tom Seaver, Juan Marichal, Dennis McLain, Jim Maloney, Don Drysdale, Jim Bunning, Hoyt Wilhelm, Sam McDowell, and Bob Gibson.

1. Pitchers (Baseball)—Biography—Juvenile literature. [1. Pitchers (Baseball)] I. Title.

GV865.A1L5 79–146652
796.357'0922 [B] [920]
MARC

Trade Edition: ISBN: 394-82112-2 Library Edition: ISBN: 394-92112-7

Manufactured in the United States of America

5/73

For Michael Leight

Acknowledgments

For their help in collecting material for this book, the author wishes to thank Harold Weissman of the New York Mets, Garry Schunacher of the San Francisco Giants, Hal Middlesworth of the Detroit Tigers, Tom Seeberg of the Cincinnati Reds, Larry Shenk of the Philadelphia Phillies, Fred Claire of the Los Angeles Dodgers, Donald Davidson of the Atlanta Braves, Ed Uhas of the Cleveland Indians, Robert Harlan of the St. Louis Cardinals, Robert Brown of the Baltimore Orioles, Charles Shriver of the Chicago Cubs, John Sheehan of the American League and Dave Grote of the National League.

33

CONTENTS

INTRODUCTION

Pitching can be a painful experience. A pitcher's arm is subjected to unnatural stresses. A pitcher also faces the pressure of being most responsible for his team's winning or losing. But each of the pitchers profiled in this book has risen above problems to be outstanding.

It is possible for a pitcher to dominate a given game of baseball as no player of any position can do in any other team sport. A football quarterback can provide points, but he needs the collaboration of receivers and he cannot stop the other side defensively. A basketball center can play offense and defense, but he cannot contain and outscore the other side by himself. A hockey goaltender can stop every shot hit at him, but he cannot score himself.

Like other key performers, a baseball pitcher needs help. He needs fielders and he needs runs if he is to win. But more than any other, a baseball pitcher can single-handedly sway a battle. He can shut out the other side, perhaps without a hit, possibly even without a base-runner. And it is possible but not probable that he could hit a homer to win the game, too.

The pitchers profiled here have not won many games with homers, but they have pitched shutouts, no-hitters, even perfect games, and won hundreds of games. Each has been chosen because he was especially outstanding in one way or another, as the reader will discover on the following pages.

STAR PITCHERS of the Major Leagues

1. TOM SEAVER

IN 1969 TOM SEAVER helped the New York Mets to a National League pennant. In previous seasons the Mets had played some of the poorest baseball in history. Their surprising pennant in 1969 was one of the great upsets in sports history. Seaver contributed by winning 25 games during the regular season and one of the Mets' three victories against Atlanta in the divisional playoffs.

The lowly Mets entered the World Series against Baltimore as underdogs. Few baseball fans expected them to provide even a fight. Seaver pitched the first game and lost. "I realized then," he said later, "how little all our accomplishments would mean if we failed at the finish." The amazing Mets rallied to win the next two games and Seaver was selected to start the fourth game. "I have never wanted to win any game more in my life," he said.

It was perhaps the crucial game of the Series. If Baltimore beat the New York pitching star a second time and evened the Series at two games apiece, they would gain considerable confidence and the Mets would be severely shaken. But if the Mets could win their third game, they would have a tremendous advantage. A capacity crowd of 57,367 fans squeezed into Shea Stadium, while television viewers across the country watched excitedly.

Only 24 years of age, the husky, handsome Californian was pitching under great pressure. He gave up a single in the first inning and a walk in the second, but avoided further trouble. Meanwhile, in the last half of the second inning, the Mets' Donn Clendenon homered off Baltimore's Mike Cuellar to give the Mets a 1-0 lead.

In the third inning, Oriole Mark Belanger singled off Seaver and Cuellar singled Belanger to second. Seaver bore down, however, and retired the next three batters in a row without a ball being hit out of the infield. In fact he retired 10 men in a row before giving up a walk in the sixth, then retired nine more.

With one out in the ninth inning, Frank Robinson singled and Boog Powell singled Robinson to third. Suddenly the Mets and Seaver, with their slim 1-0 lead, were in trouble. The next batter, Brooks Robinson, hit a sinking line drive to right-center field. The fans came to their feet screaming as Ron Swoboda dove for the ball and caught it. The runner scored from third after the catch, tying the score. Relieved that it had not been worse, Seaver pitched to Ellie Hendricks, who hit a fly to Swoboda, ending the inning. The Mets failed to score in the bottom of the ninth and the game went into extra innings.

When the Orioles came to bat in the tenth, the Mets' third baseman Wayne Garrett fumbled Dave Johnson's grounder, allowing him to reach first. With one out Dalrymple singled. A moment later Johnson reached third on a fly ball. Again Seaver was in trouble and he was tiring. But with two out he threw hard to Paul Blair and struck him out for the third out of the inning.

In the last half of the inning, pinch-hitter Joe Martin, who was batting for Seaver, came up with men on first and second. He laid down a bunt and the throw to first hit Martin on the wrist. The ball rolled into right field and the winning run scored from second. Seaver and the Mets headed for their clubhouse with a critical 2-1 victory. The Orioles' spirit was broken and the next day the Mets wrapped up their first world championship.

In the excitement of the celebration that followed, Tom Seaver said simply, "It's just the greatest thrill of my life, and I guess it would be the greatest thrill of any young man's life."

George Thomas Seaver (his wife calls him George, though sports fans know him as Tom) was born in Fresno, California, on November 17th, 1944. His father, Charles, the vice-president of a packing company, had been an outstanding golfer at Stanford. He had played on the Walker Cup team, which is one of the highest honors open to amateur golfers, and had reached the semi-finals of the U.S. amateur tournament.

During the 1969 World Series Seaver fires the ball past Baltimore's Boog Powell.

Tom was one of four children, all of whom were well provided for and encouraged to excel in sports. All four Seavers attended college and Tom's older brother and one sister were competitive swimmers. His other sister majored in physical education.

"Our family was always competitive, even working around our house," Tom has recalled. "I learned a real respect for the value of work—not for the money, but for the pleasure of doing something as well as you can. My parents were perfectionists who set very high standards for us and encouraged us to reach for the very best that was in us."

Tom became an excellent athlete. When he was 12, he pitched a perfect game in Little League play. He also batted .500 and hit ten home runs one season. His all-round ability was later an advantage in the big leagues where he became not only a superb hurler, but a good fielder and a good hitter.

Seaver's sports hero was Henry Aaron. Aaron was an outfielder and Tom was primarily a pitcher. But Aaron always was as consistent as he was spectacular and young Tom admired this especially. He used to dream of pitching to Aaron one day. And finally, one day, he did. Seaver remembers the first time well: "He hit into a double play the first time up and struck out the second time up. The third time he hit a two-run home run off me to tie the game." It was perhaps the only time in Tom's life that a rival's home run did not disappoint him. It was the sort of thing he expected from his hero.

Before Tom Seaver could become someone else's

hero, he had to grow up—in more ways than one. He had a terrible temper, for one thing. His parents both were excellent golfers and he used to play with them. When he was 12 and 13, however, he would throw his clubs when he was frustrated with his play. Eventually his mother refused to play with him any more. For awhile Seaver gave up the game. In time he learned to control his emotions.

For a long time he was handicapped by lack of size. At the age of eight he had been so small that he was cut from his first Little League tryout. He was a good basketball player, but he was only 5-foot-4 when he first attempted to make the high school varsity. He might have played football, but he weighed only 145 pounds through much of his high school career.

After graduating from high school, he went to work lifting crates of raisins at his father's company. Then he spent a six-month hitch in the Marines, during which the rugged training matured him physically. He grew to a height of 6-foot-1 and a weight of 195. Later he added about ten more pounds.

In high school he had been an ordinary baseball performer. He had some natural talent for pitching, but at 18 he was so skinny that professional baseball scouts were not especially interested in him. After leaving the service, however, he had the size to use his natural skills effectively.

In the fall of 1963 he enrolled at Fresno City College and compiled an 11-2 record for the baseball team. The University of Southern California offered

Talking to newsmen after a game, Seaver shows his winning smile.

him a scholarship for 1964-65, which he accepted, planning to study dentistry. But after he pitched for ten victories as a sophomore, pro scouts were pursuing him in earnest.

Seaver came to the Mets by an indirect route. In June of 1965 he was drafted by the Los Angeles Dodgers. But they did not offer him enough money to make him willing to discontinue his studies. This made him eligible for the next professional draft in January of 1966. This time the Atlanta Braves drafted him. When their offer reached approximately $50,000, he signed a contract with them. But by the time he signed, his USC team had played two baseball games. William Eckert, the commissioner of baseball, declared the contract void because a college student is not allowed to sign a pro contract while playing for a college team. At the same time Seaver lost his amateur status and was ineligible to play for USC because he had signed a professional contract.

Seaver appealed to the commissioner. He pointed out that he was being denied both his amateur status and a rich professional contract. Eckert agreed. He announced that any major league clubs which wished to match Atlanta's offer would be permitted to do so. The Cleveland Indians, the Philadelphia Phillies and the Mets did. Thus four teams had offered a $50,000 bonus to the young player. To decide between them, Eckert placed their names in a hat and drew one. The Mets won this strange lottery and signed Seaver immediately.

Tom was assigned to Jacksonville, Florida, of the International League, where he won 12 games and lost 12, but displayed unusual potential. He was smart, learned fast and had great poise for a youngster. He could throw hard, had practiced long and had developed exceptional control of his pitches. During spring training with the Mets in 1967, Seaver learned to throw an improved curve ball from Met pitching coach Rube Walker. Seaver was ready to reach for the top.

The Mets had begun as a new expansion team in 1962. In the five years before Seaver joined them they had finished tenth and last four times and ninth once. In Seaver's first year, 1967, they again finished tenth. However, he won 16 games and lost 13—seven of his losses by only one run—and was voted Rookie of the Year.

In mid-season he showed his unusual composure in the All-Star game. The game had been a tense pitchers' duel and was tied 1-1 after 14 innings. In the top of the 15th, the National League scored a run and Seaver was brought in in the bottom of the 15th to protect their new 2-1 lead. In this tense situation Seaver casually suggested to second baseman Pete Rose that they trade places. Of course Rose refused. Tom walked one but retired the side, assuring the Nationals' victory.

In 1968 Seaver improved his won-and-lost record slightly to 16-12 and lowered his earned-run average from 2.76 to 2.20—allowing only 2.2 earned runs to score for each nine innings pitched—thus excelling in the statistic most treasured by pitchers. The Mets, however, improved only one position, to ninth place. They continued to be the laughing-stock of baseball. They seemed to play effectively only on those days or nights their young star was pitching. Seaver went around the dressing room and suggested to his teammates, "If you can play that well behind me, you can play that well behind the other pitchers."

He became the Met cheerleader. He was a serious young man who kept himself in perfect condition and studied his profession, keeping a "book" on the habits and performances of his rival batters. But he also seemed to inspire the other Mets. "From the beginning of the 1969 season, I spoke of our team as a contender," he recalls. "This lovable loser stuff wasn't funny to me and I think it had finally stopped seeming funny to the other fellows, too."

The Mets started slowly as usual and the Chicago Cubs built a big lead in the Eastern Division. But when the Cubs began to fade, the Mets were ready. In a crucial series against the Cubs, Seaver pitched a perfect game for eight innings allowing no hits and no one to reach base. But in the ninth a light-hitting rookie, Jim Qualls, got a hit, ruining Seaver's try for the no-hitter.

"I wanted it so much, I felt chills going through me," he admitted later. "When I lost it, it was the most disappointed I've ever felt in my life." However, he retired the rest of the Cubs and won the game. When he left the dressing room that night and found his wife, Nancy, weeping, he said, "What are you crying for? A one-hit shutout isn't so bad, is it?" She smiled. He smiled. It was the Cubs who went away broken-hearted.

With their young ace winning his last 10 decisions, the Mets pulled away from the Cubs and won the pennant by a wide margin. Tom finished with a 25-7 record and a 2.21 earned run average. In the divisional playoffs he pitched one of the Mets' three straight wins over Atlanta. Then Tom and the upstart Mets completed their victorious year by

After losing his try for a no-hitter in the ninth inning against Chicago, Tom tries to explain how it happened.

winning the World Series in five games.

By the end of 1969 Tom was a celebrity. He ran second to Willie McCovey in the Most Valuable Player voting, but won the Cy Young award as the outstanding pitcher in his league and was named "Sportsman of the Year" by *Sports Illustrated* magazine. He accepted these and other awards modestly. He said, "I used to think that stepping up to receive such honors would be the ultimate, but I have found that the ultimate comes in the competition that leads to the awards."

Tom had married his college sweetheart, Nancy, and she became his biggest fan. When asked if she was jealous of his fans, she replied, "No. I want everybody to love him as much as I do." Asked what was his inspiration, his key to success, he said, "My wife." The young couple was featured in magazine articles and asked to make commercials for many different products. For the 1970 season Tom received a big salary increase from the Mets and he and Nancy moved into a large, beautiful home in Greenwich, Connecticut.

Tom started well in 1970. By midseason he had started 20 games, completed 14 and won 14. But he had pitched 172 innings and he was tiring. In the last half he won only four of 20 starts and the Mets fell to third place in their division. Seaver denied that he had a sore arm, saying that he was just tired. He often pitched well but lost close games. Although he compiled only 18 wins against twelve defeats, he still led the league in strikeouts with 283, and in earned run average with 2.81.

"If I could have pitched at the end the way I did at the beginning, I would have won 30 games," he sighed. He was disappointed and was beginning to realize that he could not be the hero of every season. Still, he remained a popular and greatly admired celebrity.

Seaver seemed uncomfortable when he was made to seem too perfect, but he admitted that he was "something of an All-American boy." He was devoted to his wife and his parents and he hoped to follow in the family tradition of helping others. His brother, who lived in New York, was a social worker. One of Tom's sisters spent two years with her husband in the Peace Corps in Nigeria. "We were taught to do for others," Seaver said. "I hope to have a good influence on young people and eventually to put any success I have had to work for good."

Seaver seemed assured of success for years to come, although a pitcher's arm is a delicate and overworked instrument. He had a smooth, compact motion and such outstanding control that he seldom wasted a pitch.

Perhaps most important to his success was his power of concentration. "I can shut everything else from my mind when I am bearing down on any one thing," he said, "and that enables me to do it better. All you owe the world and yourself is to make the best use of your talents. I am dedicated to this. Dedication and concentration are the deciding factors between who wins and who loses."

Early in 1970 Seaver turned in another record-setting performance against San Diego at Shea Stadium. He gave up two hits including a home run by Al Ferrara, but as the game progressed he began to strike out a stunning number of Padres. A teammate said, "He was like a machine. He had perfect rhythm. Whomp, whomp, whomp. Fast ball, curve ball, slider. The batters couldn't touch him. I wonder if any pitcher has ever been better."

When Ferrara took a called third strike to end the sixth inning, Seaver had his tenth strikeout. In the seventh Seaver faced Nate Colbert, Dave Campbell and Jerry Morales and struck them out. In the eighth he struck out Bob Barton, Ramon Webster and Ivan Murrell. When Van Kelly struck out on three pitches to open the ninth, Seaver had struck out eight batters in a row, tying a major league record. Three pitches later Clarence Gaston was out on a called third strike. Seaver had struck out nine straight, a new major league mark. Now he needed one more to tie the major league record for strikeouts in a single game—19.

Al Ferrara came to bat. Ferrara's homer had broken Seaver's shutout, and another now would tie the game, which stood at 2-1. But if Seaver could strike him out, he would tie another major league mark. He got two strikes on his foe. He said to himself, he confessed later, "I may never come this close again. I might as well go for it."

He gathered himself and threw the ball as hard as he could. Ferrara swung at the ball as hard as he

Al Ferrara of San Diego becomes Seaver's tenth strikeout in a row and the 19th of the game. The Met fans are overjoyed.

could—and missed. Seaver's pitch cracked into the catcher's mitt and Tom had his unprecedented tenth straight strikeout and his 19th of the game, plus a 2-1 victory.

The crowd stood and cheered as he was mobbed by his jubilant teammates. In the dressing room, the sweat streamed down his body, but he smiled broadly as he received the reporters. "Another night, another game," he smiled. Later, in a more serious mood, he said, "I did feel a sense of accomplishment, of further having proved myself."

In Tom Seaver's view, it is dangerous to make too much of yourself, important to "stay loose" and maintain your balance. In a wistful moment he once observed, "I've quickly gotten more things than lots of other people. I also know that I can lose what I have just as quickly." He concluded, "There are two parts to an outstanding champion. The first is getting there. The second is staying there." Tom Seaver is working on the second part.

2. JUAN MARICHAL

JUAN ANTONIO SANCHEZ MARICHAL (pronounced "Mar-ee-SHAL") was born October 20th, 1937, in the village of Laguna Verde in the province of Montecristi, the Dominican Republic. His family lived in a frame house with a roof thatched with banana leaves. Although the family had indoor plumbing and a gas stove, they had no electricity and little in the way of luxury.

When Juan was 3, his father died. Juan's mother wore black as a sign of mourning for more than 10 years. In the meantime she helped provide for three sons and a daughter. Everyone in the family contributed his share. As he grew up, Juan chopped sugar cane with a machete and dove for lobsters in a nearby bay.

Baseball was a favorite pastime in Laguna Verde. Juan learned it from his older brothers and played it with his friends the Alou brothers—Felipe, Matty and Jesus—all of whom later played in the major leagues. Skin-diving and spear-fishing were also pop-

Juan Marichal celebrates his 200th win in the majors after he beat the Pirates 5-1 in August 1970.

ular sports. One day when he was 12, Juan went swimming after a heavy meal and suffered stomach cramps. He struggled to shore and collapsed unconscious. He was in a coma for six days and was even pronounced dead at one point, but he recovered and grew up healthy and strong.

Many of Juan's activities revolved around baseball. He used to pretend he was a pitcher. He would line up oranges on a fence and try to knock them off with rocks. He and the Alous often made their own equipment. They made bats by cutting and trimming tree branches and drying them in the sun. They made gloves by wrapping burlap around a cardboard pattern and sewing it on with fishing line. They made balls by wrapping the center of a golf ball in the thread from a woman's stocking, sealing it with tape and getting a leather cover sewn on by a cobbler for 50 cents.

Juan's brother Garrido played semi-professional ball in neighboring communities. From Garrido Juan picked up his first pointers on how to pitch. At first Juan could only throw hard. But by the time he was 10, he could throw a sidearm curve ball and at 15 he could throw a screwball. At 17 he quit school to go to work for the United Fruit Company, which wanted him to pitch for a company team in the port town of Manzanillo. His reputation as a pitcher was spreading. Soon afterward he was drafted into the Dominican Air Force so that he could pitch for its team, which was a favorite of the Dominican dictator, Trujillo.

Juan was discharged from the service when he was 19 and was sought by American baseball scouts to sign with their teams. The Senators, the Yankees and the Dodgers spoke to Marichal. But the Giants offered him a $500 bonus and he signed a contract with the Giant organization. He was a bargain buy.

Coming to the United States in 1958, he was assigned to Michigan City, Indiana, of the Midwest League. In his first professional season he won 21 games and lost only eight. Promoted to Springfield, Massachusetts, of the Eastern League in 1959, he put together an 18-13 record in his second season. Midway in the 1960 season Juan had eleven wins and five losses with Tacoma, Washington, of the Pacific Coast League, when he was called up to play for the Giants.

Juan Marichal was only 21. But he had already shown unusual control of a wide variety of pitches. There seemed to be little left to teach him. When Juan reported to manager Bill Rigney for the first time, Rigney asked if he wanted to pitch the very next game. Juan agreed and the next day he pitched his first major league game, against Philadelphia, shutting them out on a single hit.

Marichal progressed swiftly to stardom. His record was 6-2 in his first half-season, 13-10 his first full season and 18-11 his next season. He then won 20 or more games in six of the next seven seasons with consecutive records of 25-8, 21-8, 22-13, 25-6, 14-10, 26-9 and 21-11.

In 1970 Marichal suffered from an ear infection and then from a severe allergic reaction to penicillin. It took a long time for him to regain his strength. He pitched in only 34 games and his final record was only 12-10. For a time it appeared that his career might be ended prematurely.

However, late in the season he began to regain his

rhythm and power. His victory late in August over the Pirates, 5-1, was the 200th of his career. He had joined the select group of 200-game winners and he was still only 31 years old.

"It is fun again," he smiled in the dressing room, surrounded by reporters and delighted admirers. At the end of the season, his winning percentage, .674, was the best in the history of the National League and the third best in the history of the majors. Healthy again, Marichal could look forward to many more years of success and still other records.

During his career Juan turned in many outstanding performances in individual games. One such performance came in June of 1963 against Houston. Prior to the game Juan said to teammate Willie McCovey, "I think I do something different. I change my windup and use the men-on-bases motion all the time. What you say?"

Surprised, McCovey said, "I think you're crazy. You just won five games in a row. You're pitching great your way. Why would you want to try any other way?"

"Because Houston has been hitting me a little bit. Good stuff, too," Juan explained. "Looks like they begin to figure me out. So now time to give them something else to worry about."

Usually Marichal used an elaborate motion. He reared far back, drew his right arm back almost to the ground, kicked his left leg high in the air, then uncoiled forward in a great explosion of energy. In this game he stood up straight, brought his hands together at his waist, then bent back a bit, cocked his arm and fired.

Houston batters were almost helpless. They were confused by Marichal's new motion and baffled by his fast, moving pitches. Only one of the first 14 batters was able to hit the ball out of the infield and only four were able to do so all game. There were only two sharply-hit balls off Marichal, one caught by Jim Davenport at third, the other caught by Willie McCovey in deep left field.

Through eight innings Marichal had a no-hitter. The pressure on him was especially heavy because Houston's Dick Drott was shutting out the Giants and the game was a scoreless tie. In the first half of the ninth inning the Giants' Davenport led off with a double to left. Matty Alou struck out. Marichal had a chance to win the game for himself but flied out. With two out and Davenport still on second, Chuck Hiller doubled into the right-field corner. Davenport scored and Marichal had a one-run lead.

In the last half of the ninth Houston's Johnny Temple hit a foul pop-fly near the first-base line. One out. Pinch hitter Pete Runnels came up and Marichal struck him out. Two away. Then Brock Davis stepped in. Marichal threw fast balls and screwballs, getting two strikes on him. Then he hit the corner of the plate for a called third strike. Marichal had a no-hitter. His teammates rushed to the mound to shake his hand and escort him off the field. In the dressing room he said wearily, "It is a happy time, no?"

Less than three weeks later, using his regular

windup style again, he faced the great Warren Spahn of the Braves in what Alvin Dark later called, "the best pitched game I ever saw." The game lasted four hours and ten minutes and the only run of the game was recorded when the Giants' Willie Mays homered in the 16th inning to give Juan the win, 1-0.

It was not unusual for Marichal to finish what he started. In one five-year stretch he completed 90 percent of the games he won, a remarkable record in an age of great relief pitchers. In 1968 Juan pitched 30 complete games, one of the best single-season marks in modern history.

Marichal had many things going for him. He overpowered batters with his awesome motion and kept them guessing with his great variety of pitches. Opposing players argued about the number of different pitches he could throw. Some said 20. Some said 40. He may have had even more. Marichal had a fast ball, curve, change-up, screwball, slider, slip-pitch and palm-ball. He threw each of these overhand, three-quarters-arm and sidearm and he threw them at at least four different speeds, giving him more than 80 possible combinations.

The fast ball remained a basic pitch for Marichal. Rival Tom Haller once said, "Marichal throws so hard he could pitch his fast ball through a carwash and not get it wet." However, Marichal himself said, "My control is most responsible for my success."

Marichal shows his spectacular pitching form. He lifts his leg far above his head, then brings the ball around from far behind his body.

Ballplayers said of him, "He pitches on the black." When a new home plate is unwrapped, it has a thin black fringe on its sides. While he threw more strikes than most pitchers, he threw them not across the center of the plate but across the corners and edges where the batters found them difficult to judge. He struck out as many as 248 batters a season and walked as few as 62.

Although Juan was plagued by a variety of injuries and ailments, he still was the most durable of modern pitchers, averaging 40 starts, 25 complete games and 300 innings pitched each season. He was also the most consistent winner in recent years. Many recent pitchers have won 20 games once or twice, but only Marichal has come close to *averaging* 20 wins per season over ten years or more.

For all of this, the spectacular star received remarkably little recognition. He never won the Most Valuable Player award in his league nor the Cy Young award as the best pitcher. He received less attention from writers and fans than a Sandy Koufax or a Dennis McLain, even though his career record was far more impressive. Juan had the misfortune each year of being overshadowed by one or two pitchers whose accomplishments in that season were remarkable. Marichal never matched Koufax's record for strikeouts or McLain's 31 wins, but he was winning steadily before they were well-known and it seemed possible that he would outlast them both. Another reason that Marichal was seldom in the limelight was that the Giants usually finished second.

The Giants won a pennant only in Marichal's second season, 1962, and he suffered an injured finger that limited his play in his only World Series.

Marichal gained a reputation as a moody person. The round-faced, handsome Latin had an appealing smile and was never involved in a scandal off the field, but he often seemed to stand apart from his fellow players and the baseball writers. His image was severely stained by an incident on the playing field in 1965 when he struck Los Angeles Dodger catcher John Roseboro with a bat.

The incident grew out of a "beanball war," in which players on both sides accused opposing pitchers of throwing at batters' heads. The Dodgers and the Giants were battling for the pennant late in the season and tempers were hot. While Marichal was at bat, Roseboro threw close to his head while returning the ball to his pitcher. Marichal said something to Roseboro about it. Roseboro replied and they headed for each other. Marichal raised his bat and clubbed Roseboro on the head.

The umpires and the players from both sides converged on home plate, separating the combatants and pushing and shoving one another. A full riot almost began but order finally was restored. Marichal was ejected from the game while Roseboro had to be treated for scalp injuries. Newspapers were filled with stories and pictures of the incident, and photos of a bleeding Roseboro drew considerable sympathy. Marichal drew a great deal of criticism.

Juan was fined $1,750 and suspended for eight

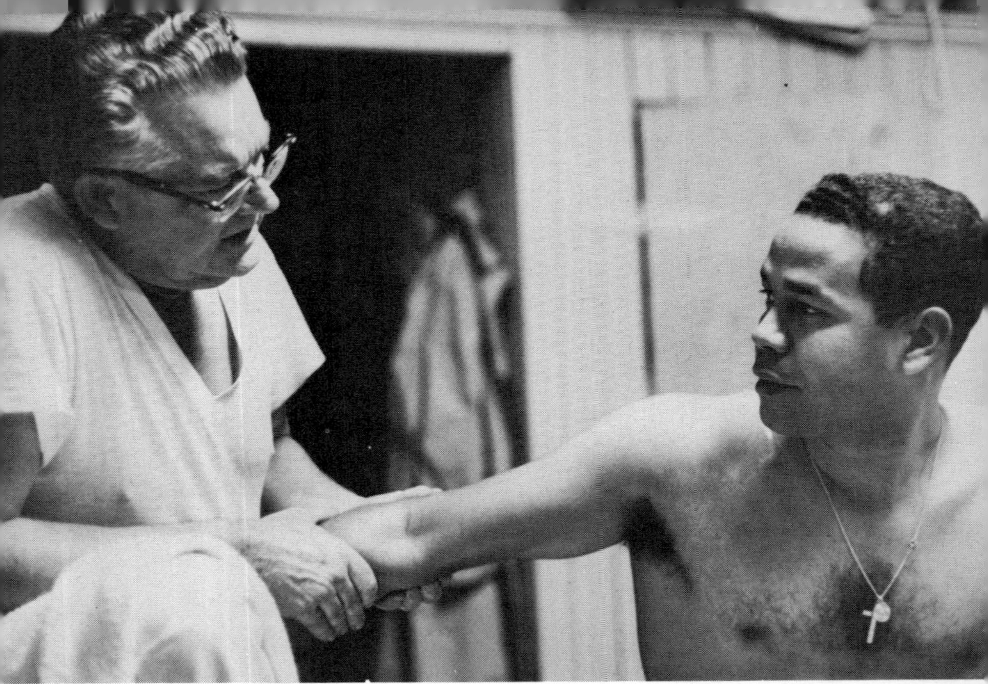

The Giant trainer works out the kinks in Marichal's arm before a game.

playing days by National League president Warren Giles. Many considered this punishment too light. Roseboro later sued Marichal and eventually settled for $7,500, most of which was paid by the Giant management.

Recalling the incident later, Marichal explained, "The ball ticked my right ear. I think Roseboro was trying to start a fight with me. He had on a face mask and chest protector, so I couldn't hit him with my hands. I lost my temper for a moment. I am sorry I hit him, but I do feel he asked for it."

Like many Latin baseball players, Marichal never seemed to feel completely at home in the United States. He had to learn a new language, play with mostly English-speaking Americans, and live in what was for him a foreign land. There were hints that many Latin players, including Marichal, felt they had suffered from prejudice as much or more than black Americans.

Marichal often complained that he was not paid as well as American superstars, although he was one of the first athletes to earn $100,000 or more a season. He invested his money carefully in the Dominican Republic and eventually owned more than 1,000 acres of land.

His mother and sister lived on the Marichal ranch, and Juan and his wife, Alma Rosa, whom he married in 1962, returned to it each winter. They raised beans, rice and corn. The ranch was maintained by a full-time staff of ten or more. Juan was proud of his ranch and proud that he treated his employees well. When he was home, he bred horses and fighting cocks and spear-fished in coral lagoons.

Although many in the Dominican Republic resented Juan's leaving to seek his fortune in the United States, they soon became proud of his success in baseball and of his continuing interest in his native land. He became something of a hero and has received the kind of admiration at home that he had not received in the United States.

Marichal was also a religious person. For many years, whenever he returned to his homeland, he made a pilgrimage to the church of La Virgen Altagracia, pausing to bathe briefly in the "holy waters" of the River Sanate on his way. Marichal was troubled with back problems for years and when they finally disappeared, he attributed his cure to the assistance of the Virgin.

Marichal's affection for his homeland and his occasional resentment of the United States seemed strange to those who considered baseball the American game. But Juan had overcome many handicaps and worked hard and consistently toward becoming one of baseball's great performers. When he has retired to become a rancher in the Dominican Republic, he will keep his place on the list of all-time great pitchers and he may someday return to see his plaque placed in baseball's Hall of Fame.

3. DENNIS McLAIN

THERE ARE TWO DAYS that stand out in Dennis McLain's career. One came on a Saturday in September of 1968, when Dennis pitched for his Tigers in Detroit against the Oakland Athletics.

Denny awakened at 9 that morning and relaxed for a while in his basement, playing his Hammond Organ. He had a breakfast of eggs, sausage and Pepsi Cola. Soon the phone began ringing. Writers and broadcasters wanted to know what he was doing and thinking and how he was feeling. Denny had won 29 games in the 1968 season. Fans all over the country were interested in his try for a 30th win—a feat which no one had accomplished in 34 years.

The pressure on Denny had been building for weeks. Reporters wanted interviews. Business agents and publicity men pursued him to seek his endorsement of a product or financial support for a new project. Denny was only 24 and the pressure was beginning to tell on him. On this day he left early for Tiger Stadium. At the ballpark, at least, he felt he could concentrate on baseball. But today more writers, more agents and more publicists were waiting for him when he arrived.

Sandy Koufax, perhaps the greatest pitcher of the 1960s, was there. So was Dizzy Dean, who had won 30 games in 1934. McLain shook hands and answered questions and accepted good wishes. Finally he went out to warm up. Almost everyone except the opposition seemed to want Denny to win, but the game turned out to be a struggle.

In the fourth inning, with one man on base, Oakland's Reggie Jackson hit one of McLain's curve balls into the stands to give the A's a 2-0 lead. The crowd groaned. Later Denny said ruefully, "It was a good pitch." Tiger Norm Cash hit a three-run homer to give Detroit the lead. But the A's came back to tie the game. Then Jackson hit a high changeup pitch for another homer to put Oakland ahead 4-3. The fans groaned again. "It was my only bad pitch," Denny said later.

When the Tigers came up in the last of the ninth, they were still behind 4-3. It seemed that McLain had lost the game. But pinch-hitter Al Kaline walked and Mickey Stanley singled him to third. Jim Northrup topped a grounder to first. The A's Danny Cater fielded it and threw to home in an attempt to get Kaline. But the throw flew over the catcher's head—Kaline was home safe and the game was tied. Willie Horton then drove the ball past the left fielder and Stanley came home with the winning run.

The fans went wild. McLain's teammates escorted

Denny McLain is surrounded by sportswriters and well-wishers after winning his 30th game of the 1968 season.

him through the crowd, which had already rushed onto the field, and into the dressing room. There, TV, radio and newspaper men were waiting for the first interviews. Outside, the fans continued to roar. Approximately 10,000 remained in the stands chanting, "We want Denny! We want Denny! We want Denny!" Finally, tired but smiling, McLain was led through the dark tunnel back to the dugout. The moment he stepped onto the field, a thunderous roar went up. He stopped still, seemingly amazed at the ovation he was receiving.

He had not been an overly popular player until

then. He frequently had criticized his teammates and the writers and fans in Detroit, but with his historic triumph, all was forgiven. He began to wave to the fans, his smile growing wider as he went toward the mound.

"Look at this, will ya?" he said to those who were with him. "Look at those people. I can't believe it."

Finally he headed back through the tunnel to the dressing room where the television cameras awaited him. "That's the greatest thrill I've ever had in my life. Those people out there—they're fantastic," he said.

He had pitched his team to the brink of its first pennant in more than 20 years and would soon lead them into the World Series. At the same time he had become the most famous and acclaimed athlete in the country, on the verge of great glory and riches.

Less than two years later McLain faced another big day. He had been suspended from baseball for the first three months of the 1970 season for associating with gamblers. His finances were in such disorder that he was unable to pay his bills and had been forced to declare bankruptcy.

Now, on the first of July, 1970, his suspension had been lifted and he was about to pitch his first game of the season, facing the New York Yankees in Detroit. Every seat in the ballpark had been sold out long in advance for the game. Nearly 54,000 fans were in Tiger Stadium to see his comeback attempt.

Again McLain had faced fierce pressure from newsmen and others before the game. Since he had not been permitted to train with his team, he had been working out on his own. Although he said he was in shape, there was an uncertainty in his manner which had not been there before.

For one thing, he did not know how the fans would receive him. It did not take him long to find out. He received three ovations right at the beginning—one when he took the field to warm up, another when he took the mound to start the game, and a third when his name was announced in the introductions. He smiled and nodded his head and even tipped his cap. He seemed shy, where before he had seemed so brash and sure of himself.

He also remained uncertain about his ability to pitch well. He was the Denny McLain of two years earlier in some respects. He still wore his hat cocked at a jaunty angle. He still walked back and forth from the dugout slowly, pounding his glove all the way. He still had his peculiar, stiff-legged delivery. But when the game began, the ball did not behave for him as it once had.

He could not throw as hard as before. His breaking pitches did not break as well. His control was off. He struggled from the start. First the Yankees' Jerry Kenney hit a home run off him. Then Thurmon Munson hit one. Then Bobby Murcer hit one. McLain trailed, 5-3, when manager Mayo Smith relieved him in the sixth inning. The Tigers rallied to win later, but McLain received none of the credit.

Afterwards Denny said that during the first ovation, which had lasted a full minute, he had almost cried. "I'm not an emotional man, but it was hard to hold myself together when I heard those cheers," he admitted. But after his poor performance, the newsmen were not so eager to talk to him. When Denny left the ballpark later, only a few fans were waiting to greet him.

McLain's comeback was much tougher than he expected it to be. It took three weeks and six starts before he won his first game. The victories continued to come slowly and only with a struggle as the last half of the season wore on. On his return he had seemed sincerely humble and eager to atone for any mistakes he might have made off the field. However, as his pitching problems mounted, he seemed to grow impatient and irritable.

He had won only three games and lost five when his season came to an abrupt end. At the end of August he doused some sportswriters with a bucket of water and was suspended again, this time by the Tigers. He laughingly explained his behavior as a mere prank but the Tigers were not amused. Just when they reinstated him, Denny was suspended again by the baseball commissioner for carrying a gun and other "conduct detrimental to baseball."

When the season ended, Detroit traded McLain to Washington. The Washington owner, Bob Short, hoped that McLain would attract more fans to the games. But others with the team were not overjoyed that the problem pitcher would soon be their teammate. The fortunes of the still-young star had taken another sharp dip.

Dennis Dale McLain was born March 29th, 1944, in suburban Chicago. He grew up to be an extroverted young man and a talented athlete. His attitude toward life may have been shaped more than anything else by the death of his father, Tim. The elder McLain, who had taught Denny how to pitch and play the organ, died of a heart attack at the age of 36 while on his way to watch Denny pitch in a high school game.

"I walked all over town and cried all day," Denny recalled years later. "But I haven't cried since then. No tears in my eyes since I was 15. I was young to be alone, my kid brother and I, and I didn't want to be frightened. I made myself hard."

He worked as a supermarket checker five nights a week while continuing his musical studies and baseball play. "I was insecure," he said later. "We didn't have any money. I always thought it was terrible not to have any money. I wanted to be rich. The richer the better."

The red-haired youngster was a fiery competitor on the ball field for Mount Carmel High School. He frequently was thrown out of games for arguing. But he has said of these arguments. "I was always right. I still am." A compulsive talker, Denny always found it difficult to admit being wrong.

His high school pitching record was 38-7, even though he threw almost all fastballs. He had a strong arm and seemed to be able to throw hard all day. In 1962 he was signed by the Chicago White Sox for a $17,000 bonus. His first professional start was about as promising as any on record—he pitched a no-hitter for Harlan, Kentucky, in the Appalachian League. He was swiftly promoted to Clinton, Iowa, in the Midwest League, where he had a 4-7 mark.

In his first year McLain was promising, but he was also unreliable. He broke curfew many nights and frequently was fined. Several times he became discouraged with his teams and just packed up and went home. The White Sox lost interest in him and failed to protect him from the major league draft of minor league players in 1963. Detroit claimed him for $8,000, which turned out to be a bargain although it bought them headaches, too.

McLain spent the 1963 season in Duluth-Superior of the Northern League, where his record was 13-2, and Knoxville of the Sally League, where he was 5-4. He was brought up briefly to pitch for the Tigers, winning two and losing one. He began 1964 in Syracuse of the International League, going 3-1, but then was called up to Detroit and the majors, where he remained from then on.

McLain learned quickly. He picked up valuable pointers from Charley Dressen, the Tiger manager, and pitching coach Johnny Sain. He developed a classic style with a high, easy kick and a rhythmic motion. He always could throw hard and soon developed a good large curve and small curve, called a "slider," all of which he could throw overarm or sidearm. As he mastered his control, which took a few seasons, he became consistently effective.

Mayo Smith, who became the Detroit manager,

said the secret to McLain's success was his concentration and his competitive spirit. "He really bears down on every batter." Added Detroit catcher Bill Freehan, "What he has more than anything else is guts. He's not afraid to challenge the best."

McLain himself said, "I enjoy pitching. It's never work for me. If I have my good stuff, I'll go after everybody right away. If my stuff is mediocre in a given game, I'll keep the ball away from them and work on them carefully. Pitching is a science. The secret is to make the batter swing at what he least wants to hit. I relax off the field, but I bear down on the mound."

He was only 4-5 the last half of 1964. But early in 1965 he showed signs of things to come. In a game against Boston he came in in relief, struck out the first seven batters he faced and then struck out seven more before the game was over. He was soon taken out of the bullpen and made a starter. He won eight games in a row and wound up with a 16-6 record. The next season, only his second full season in the big time, he became a 20-game winner, going 20-14. In 1967 he won 17 and lost 16.

Then in 1968 he burst through with his season of seasons. Denny won two games in April, six in May, six in June, seven in July. His 20th victory late in July was a three-hit 9-0 shutout of Baltimore. Writers and fans began to speculate that he might win 30. In August McLain won five out of six decisions and in September five of six for a season total of 31.

In his last win of the season an incident occurred

McLain seems to be all alone on the field as he fires a pitch toward the plate.

that illustrated his casual attitude toward life. At that point Mickey Mantle was tied for third among all-time home-run hitters with 534. At bat Mickey motioned to McLain that he would like a fast ball across the chest. Denny fired a fast ball across the chest and Mantle hit it into the stands. McLain actually joined the fans in applauding him. Mickey yelled "thanks" as he rounded third. Later McLain smilingly denied that he had deliberately fed Mantle a soft pitch. "I give up a lot of home runs," he

said, grinning. "I don't think one more makes any difference."

McLain did give up too many home runs, but his other statistics in 1968 were remarkable. He started 41 games, completed 12 and had an incredible record of 17-2 away from home, where many pitchers lose more often. Playing no favorites, McLain defeated every rival team both at home and on the road. He led the league by pitching 336 innings, set a Detroit team record with 280 strikeouts and had a splendid 1.96 earned run average.

McLain received the Cy Young award as the outstanding pitcher in the American League and became the first pitcher in the league since 1952 to win the Most Valuable Player trophy. Both awards are given by the baseball writers and McLain was their unanimous choice both times.

His only disappointment in 1968 was his performance against St. Louis in the World Series. In the first game he gave up three runs in five innings and lost to Bob Gibson, who struck out 17 Tigers. In the fourth game he gave up four runs and was knocked out in the third inning. The Tigers went on to lose, 10-1. But McLain came through in the sixth game. He scattered nine hits in pitching a 3-1 victory that squared the series at three victories each. The Tigers, led by pitcher Mickey Lolich, won the seventh game and the World Championship.

McLain looked forward to 1969 as a chance to prove that his success was no fluke. He was troubled by a sore shoulder and required pain-killing injections of cortisone, but he still demonstrated his greatness. He led the league in innings pitched with 325; in starts with 41; in complete games with 23; and in victories with 24. He lost only nine games and pitched nine shutouts. He shared the Cy Young laurels with Baltimore's Mike Cuellar and became the youngest active pitcher with 100 victories in his career.

But his personal problems were beginning to get in the way of his success. Denny had always been cocky. Almost as soon as he joined the Tigers he said, "I want to make a lot of money." He had always asked for enormous increases in his salary. He also said, "I'm aggressive at everything. With a year's practice I could go on the pro golf tour. I think I could be a pro quarterback. God knows I can throw the ball." His teammates called him "Mighty Mouth" and "Super Flake."

In 1969 he called the Tigers "a country club team" and the Detroit fans "the worst fans in baseball, nothing but front-runners." Someone put a smoke bomb in the engine of his car, which went off when his wife stepped on the accelerator, scaring her terribly. Denny was angry about this, but as his victories mounted, his earlier comments were forgotten, he was cheered and his attitude toward his fans softened.

With success, however, he seemed to grow irresponsible. He came and went as he pleased, practicing only when he wished. He was seldom reprimanded by the manager or by his bosses, and his teammates resented the special treatment he received. Many of the Tigers remembered that Denny had been unable to pitch in the last weeks of 1967 when the Tigers had lost a pennant. Denny had been sidelined with a sore foot which had been injured under mysterious circumstances. Many of his teammates felt his outside interests were distracting him from his responsibilities to the team.

McLain was married to the former Sharyn Boudreau, the daughter of Lou Boudreau, a member of

McLain's expression tells the story of his 1970 season as he gives up a home run to Baltimore's Boog Powell (left) and another to Ellie Hendricks (right). Baltimore won 13-3.

baseball's Hall of Fame who had played and managed for the Cleveland Indians for 17 seasons. Denny and Sharyn had a daughter and two adopted sons, but Denny seldom was home. "I hate to sleep. You only live once and I'm afraid I'm going to miss something," he said. He played the organ in night clubs across the country and became involved in many business deals. He bought his own plane so he could keep his busy schedule.

But his many interests became too much to manage. By 1969 many of his business interests were collapsing. Although he reportedly had been earning $200,000 a year he admitted "I'm broke." Knowingly or unknowingly he had invested $5,700 in a gambling operation conducted in Flint, Michigan. Baseball Commissioner Bowie Kuhn suspended him for the first three months of the 1970 season for conduct detrimental to the sport. He was put on his "best behavior" and told to straighten out his affairs.

At a press conference after the suspension was announced, a writer said to McLain, "Commissioner Kuhn said you were gullible and avaricious. Do you agree?"

"I'm afraid I'd have to get a dictionary before answering," McLain said.

"It means you were stupid and greedy," a writer said.

McLain paused, then said, "Yes, I was stupid and greedy."

His plane and some other holdings were repossessed. He filed bankruptcy papers. He turned his business affairs over to Mark McCormack, a lawyer who had successfully represented other athletes. As the time for his return grew near, he admitted, "Once something is taken away from you, you find out what it means to you." He insisted, however, as he had insisted all along, "I've never done anything to hurt baseball."

On his return he walked into the Tiger clubhouse and announced, "Boys, you are seeing the new Denny McLain." He made up with his catcher, Bill Freehan, who had written unfavorably about him. Still as playful as ever, McLain met with Freehan in the trainer's room prior to his return to the mound and made a lot of noise, simulating a fight to tease newsmen. Suddenly McLain opened the door and sent a bucketful of ice-water gushing through, hoping to trap a reporter who was eavesdropping. The water hit trainer Bill Behm, not a reporter.

Later in the year he was suspended first for another ice-water incident and then for other misbehavior. He was only 26 years old and already he was struggling to live up to his earlier accomplishments. Although he was still a pitcher of rare promise, his problems off the field made his future very uncertain. It seemed possible that he would turn out to be a gifted young man who could not handle success. Only time would tell.

4. JIM MALONEY

THE HUMAN ARM is a delicate piece of equipment and the baseball pitcher subjects it to severe stresses. By snapping it hard, stretching it and twisting it to throw breaking pitches, he abuses it. After a full nine innings of pitching, the arm may begin to bleed internally. Small muscle tears develop. As the tears heal, scar-tissue develops. Small pieces of scar tissue, no larger than grains of salt, sometimes flake off and rub and irritate the surrounding flesh forever after, causing what is known as a sore arm, a common pitchers' complaint.

Jim Maloney suffered from sore arms from the time his pitching career began. Like many other pitchers, he had to pack his arm in ice or bathe it in ice-water for as long as a full hour after pitching a long game to promote healing and reduce swelling. Like many other pitchers, he had to pitch in pain. Sandy Koufax and Don Drysdale are other pitchers who nursed their arms through serious injuries and often pitched in pain. By the end of the 1960s, both

Koufax and Drysdale had retired, their careers cut short, but Maloney still struggled on.

Maloney broke into the major leagues with Cincinnati in 1960. "My pitching arm has hurt most of the time since," he once admitted. "It hurts mainly at the shoulder. I take cortisone shots to relieve the pain and I do the best I can. Sometimes this has been very good. When my arm doesn't feel too bad, I can win three or four out of every five starts. When it is at its worst, the best I can do is break even. Still, I can't go around thinking what I could have done if the arm wasn't always sore. There are some things you have to accept. This is one of them."

The 6-foot-2, 200-pound right-hander had a heavily-muscled body. Cincinnati trainer Bill Cooper, who spent long hours massaging Maloney's arm to stretch and loosen the muscles before his pitching assignments, once said, "Maloney is too muscular. Instead of stretching his muscles when he pitches, he rips them. As he gets older, these tears don't heal as fast as they used to. It gets increasingly harder for veterans like Maloney to carry on, but this is their profession and they do it."

Often before a game, the team doctor stuck a long needle loaded with cortisone into Maloney's shoulder and wiggled it around until the point was in the most inflamed area. Then he released the relief-giving fluid. This, of course, was only a temporary cure, but if Maloney was to continue in baseball, there was no alternative. But for all of his physical problems, the big, powerful, hard-throwing veteran had unusual success.

At his best, Jim was one of the best. He pitched three no-hitters. Only Sandy Koufax, with four to his credit, ever pitched more. Through the end of the 1960s Maloney also had pitched five one-hitters and nine two-hitters. When Maloney was right, no one pitched faster and few could break off curves more sharply. He was simply stunning in his most overpowering moments.

In 1965 he became one of only four pitchers ever to hurl two no-hit games in the same season. It was Maloney's luck that both games went into extra innings and that he actually lost one of them. In June of 1965 he pitched no-hit ball against the New York Mets for ten innings, but the Reds had not scored and he was still locked in a scoreless tie. In the first half of the 11th inning, Met rookie Johnny Lewis, a .250 hitter, hit a towering home run that won the game for the Mets, 1-0. Maloney also gave up a single to Roy McMillan before retiring the side to settle for a two-hitter, though he was officially credited with a 10-inning no-hitter.

Thus Maloney was a loser despite what the Reds' pitching coach Jim Turner called, "The finest pitching performance I've ever seen." Catcher Johnny Edwards later summed up the Reds' frustration by saying, "I'd have crawled home on my hands and knees to give him the winning run." Manager Dick Sisler said, "It was a dirty shame."

After the game he sat slumped in the dressing room, sweat pouring off him, and said, "I was aware

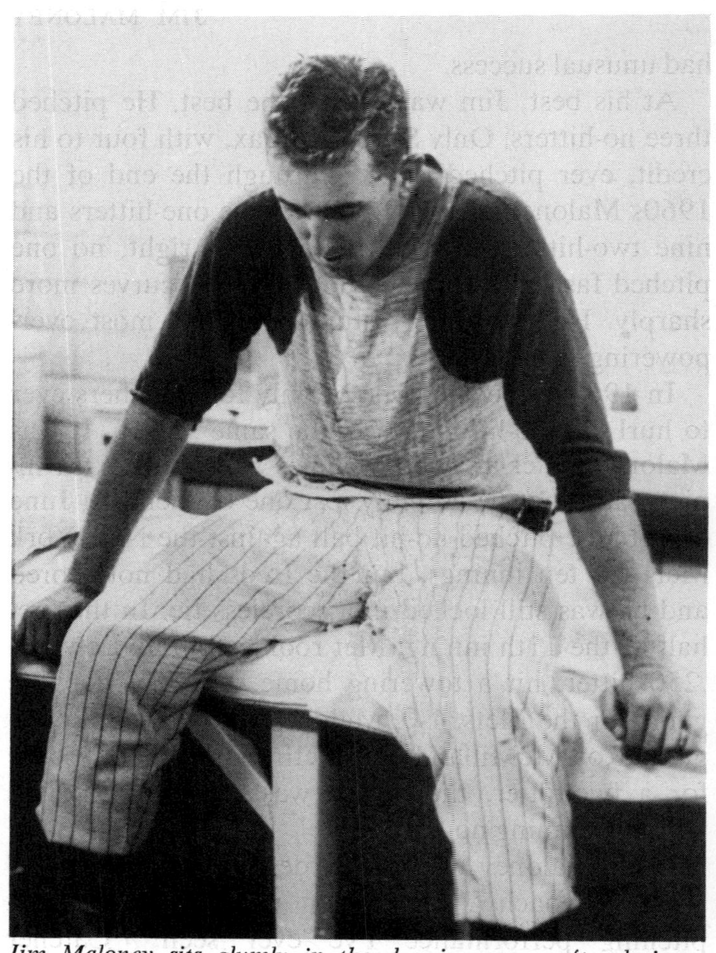

Jim Maloney sits glumly in the dressing room after losing a no-hit game by giving up a home run in the 11th inning.

of the no-hitter, of course, and I wanted it very much, but the longer it went on, the greater was the chance I'd let a pitch get away from me. I tried to pitch inside to Lewis, but the pitch got out over the plate and he kissed it goodbye."

Lewis had struck out three times previously in the game. He admitted, "No one ever threw harder to me. I just got lucky." In all, the luckless Maloney struck out 18 Mets in the 11-inning contest, as many as any pitcher ever had struck out in a single game. Although he was often wild, in this game he walked only one. No one had even come close to getting a clean hit until Lewis' home run.

Earlier in the season Maloney had lost a one-hitter he had tossed against the San Francisco Giants and Juan Marichal. But losing a no-hitter was much more heartbreaking. He sat sadly by his locker for a long time before he went to shower. Finally he hoisted himself wearily to his feet. "These things usually have a way of balancing out," he said philosophically. "Perhaps another time when I need a break to win, I'll get it."

In August, just two months later, Maloney was pitching another no-hitter, this time against the Chicago Cubs in Chicago's Wrigley Field. When he came to bat in the eighth, Cub catcher Ed Bailey said to him, "You look pretty good, but we might knock one out of the park on you."

Maloney just grinned and said, "You may be right. It wouldn't surprise me after what's happened to me before." Although the game was still 0-0 after nine innings, this time Maloney got his break. In the first half of the tenth inning, Leo Cardenas, the little Red shortstop, hit a home run. The drive landed just barely to the fair side of the left-field foul pole. Maloney leaped to his feet and rushed out to welcome Cardenas as he crossed the plate.

The big pitcher still had to go out to the mound under awesome pressure to complete his no-hitter. He succeeded, thus becoming one of the few men ever to complete a 10-inning no-hit victory and the only man in history ever to pitch two 10-inning no-hitters.

In some ways this no-hitter was less artistic than the one he lost. Maloney had walked 10 Cubs and hit one batter. He threw 187 pitches, enough for two full games. Fourteen times he went to 3-and-2 counts on a batter but in nine of these situations he had gotten them out. The Cubs were awed by the wild fireballer. They did not hit a ball out of the infield until the eighth inning and they did not come close to a hit at any time.

"I had 'em terrified," he grinned later. But he added with relief, "I was the most frightened guy on the ball field. I really didn't want to lose this one. I wasn't sure I'd get another one."

But he did get another chance at a no-hitter four seasons later, in April of 1969, against the Houston Astros in Cincinnati. He had the comfort of a cushion in this one, stifling the Astros on five walks and no hits in a 10-0 triumph. Jim drove in the Reds' ninth run in the eighth inning, then he scored the final run, running through a third base coach's "stop sign" and pulling a groin muscle in the process. Despite his discomfort, he retired the side in order in the ninth.

Maloney throws hard as the shortstop and the umpire watch.

"When I have it, I'm pretty hard to hit," a delighted Maloney conceded later. Unfortunately for him and fortunately for his foes, Maloney did not always have it. If he had, he might have compiled a career record better than any before.

James William Maloney was born June 2nd, 1940, in Fresno, California. His father Tim, an auto-dealer there, was a huge and powerful man, whose nickname was "Hands" because of his strong grip. He had played semi-pro football and also service baseball.

Jim had a sister who later became a schoolteacher in San Diego. But he was an only son and his father shared his own keen interest in sports with the boy. "Dad started me out. He taught me the fundamentals. He gave me a love for sports," Jim says.

In Little League ball Jim was a shortstop who hit hard and threw well. Occasionally he played the outfield or pitched. Maloney attended Fresno High School, where Tom Seaver was to go a few years later. In Maloney's years there Dick Ellsworth was Fresno's star pitcher. When he graduated, Ellsworth signed a $75,000 bonus contract with the Chicago Cubs. Maloney, who had remained at shortstop and hit .500 in his senior year, enrolled at Fresno City College.

Jim did have tryouts as a shortstop with Baltimore and Cincinnati and had considered signing with them for modest sums. However, his dad had a strong feeling that his son's future hopes lay in pitching and that Jim would get a shot at mound stardom.

Jim remembers listening with his father to a radio account of an exhibition game in which bonus baby Ellsworth shut out the White Sox, 1-0. Afterwards his dad said, "Son, if Dick can pitch against a major league team like that, you have to try it."

In his first year at Fresno City, Maloney tried pitching. He was a sensation. At one stage he pitched 19 consecutive hitless innings. By then major league scouts were pursuing him and 16 major league teams made him offers. In April of 1959 he signed with Cincinnati for the same sum, $75,000, that had been paid his teammate Ellsworth.

He broke in with Topeka, Kansas, with six victories and seven defeats. He was good in spots but wild and inconsistent. The next season he moved up to Nashville in the Southern Association and overpowered his foes while running up a 14-5 record. He was promptly called up to Cincinnati, but he remained wildly inconsistent and finished the season winning only two and losing six.

In 1961 he spent the full season with Cincinnati but was used sparingly and settled for a mediocre 6-7 mark. Injured in spring training the following year, he was assigned to San Diego of the Pacific Coast League, which shook him up. "I learned that I couldn't last nine innings just by standing out there on the mound and humming the fast ball," he recalls.

He developed his curve ball and change-up, won four out of five decisions and won another chance

After pitching his third no-hitter, Maloney is carried off the field on his teammates' shoulders.

with Cincinnati, where he won nine of 16 decisions. By 1963 he had gained sufficient control of his blazing fast ball and other stuff to post a 23-7 record and 265 strikeouts, which still stand as his single-season highs. In one game, against the Milwaukee Braves, he struck out 16 batters, the third highest in history to that time, including eight in a row.

In 1964 he began to suffer from a sore arm and struggled to season records of 15-10, 20-9, 16-8, 15-11, 16-10 and 12-5. In 1970 he sat out most of the season with a ruptured tendon in one foot and gained a mere 0-1 mark. This was ironic, for he was the only remaining Red from the team that had won the pennant in 1961. After years of pitching powerfully under great handicaps for poor clubs, he was unable to contribute to the improved team's victory in the National League. He was sorely missed in the World Series which the Reds lost to Baltimore.

For all of his troubles, he had won 134 games in ten full seasons, and at 30 he was not yet willing to give up. "I can't kick," he said in the Cincinnati clubhouse after a game in 1970. "I consider myself successful. I've fought off physical troubles for years and I figure I may be able to do so for awhile longer yet. Next year is a new slate. Next year is always a new slate."

He sat by himself, seemingly alienated by his physical problems from his healthy, happy, hot teammates. "I would have liked to have contributed more to them," he admitted. "I don't know if they understand what this thing has been for me. All this time it was the arm. Now the foot. I doubt that they believe in me."

Maloney had spent his major league career with one team. He was married and had two daughters. Yet the tall, dark veteran never settled down. "We rent an apartment. We never felt secure enough to buy a house," he said wistfully. "Baseball is a very insecure life. Any sport is. Over the years, most of my teammates and friends have been traded, sold or released. I had no idea I would stay put all this time. And with my arm trouble I could not have guessed

I'd last this long. Great pitchers like Koufax and Drysdale have had to give up. I've just found it hard to do."

In December of 1970 Jim was traded to the California Angels, ending his eleven-year connection with Cincinnati. It would be difficult for him to start over again but it would not be easy for him to give up. He had been too good too many times. He averaged more than eight strikeouts every nine innings, second only to Koufax. He averaged less than eight hits given up every nine innings. Only eight pitchers have averaged less. He had those no-hitters and one-hitters and two-hitters. Despite the pain, he had pitched his way to success.

5. DON DRYSDALE

THROUGHOUT MOST OF HIS CAREER Don Drysdale received slim support from his Los Angeles Dodgers. Sometimes it seemed he had to pitch a shutout to win. But often Drysdale was so strong a pitcher that he needed only the barest support. In 1968 he showed his strength as no pitcher in the history of the major leagues ever had.

On May 14th in Los Angeles Don stopped the Chicago Cubs on two hits, 4-0. Four nights later he stifled the Houston Astros on five hits, 1-0. On May 22nd Drysdale subdued the Cardinals in St. Louis on five hits, 2-0. Then four nights later he tamed the Astros again, in Houston, on six hits, 5-0.

The last one came hard. Drysdale, sometimes known as the Big Warrior, permitted four men to reach base in the ninth inning on two hits, a hit batter and a walk. But a double play kept a run from scoring. He got the last out on a ground ball with the bases loaded. "I don't think I could have thrown even one more pitch," he admitted later.

Don Drysdale (right) talks with his teammate Sandy Koufax in 1965. Drysdale's accomplishments were often overshadowed by Sandy's until Koufax retired in 1966.

Drysdale flew home to rest up so he could open the next home stand against his team's traditional rivals, the league-leading San Francisco Giants. He already had tied the National League record of four straight shutouts set by Mordecai "Three-Finger" Brown of the Chicago Cubs in 1908 and equalled by four other pitchers.

As he dressed for the game, Don had his sights set on the major league mark of five straight shutouts set by "Doc" White of the Chicago White Sox in 1904. "You need luck to pitch any shutout," he said. "It doesn't take much of a mistake to bring in a run. I've been pitching well and with good luck. I don't know how long this streak can last. The big thing is consistency—giving up as few runs as possible every game, game after game.

"I think sometimes a lot of hitters are stupid. They play into pitchers' hands. Young hitters come up swinging from the end of the stick for home runs, 165-pounders who think they're Mickey Mantles. I'd rather face a free-swinger any time rather than a smart hitter who just tries to hit the ball where it's pitched, to meet it solidly."

He took his swings in batting practice, loosening up. Then he clattered back down the runway on his spikes to a small room where a trainer massaged his right arm. Don lay quietly on a long table, listening to rock-and-roll music blaring out of a loudspeaker. Then he got up and picked a piece of bubblegum from a box. He walked back out to the dugout and sat down to wait the last long minutes before the game started. He was a strikingly handsome man with tanned skin and light brown hair, a big man with an imposing appearance. Now, with night falling and the stadium filling with excited fans, Drysdale waited for his chance at immortality and blew bubbles.

When it was time to take the mound, he walked out and tipped his cap as the fans applauded him. He began to warm up, pitching in his rare individual style. He raised his left knee, pivoted far around, cocked his right wrist far back, then uncoiled, whipping the ball sidearm toward the plate. He could throw hard and he was not afraid to throw close to the batters. His pitches seemed to batters to come from somewhere near third base.

As the game began, the Giants seemed tense. Ron Hunt flied out. Jim Davenport singled, but Willie Mays struck out swinging and Willie McCovey bounced out. Another shutout inning had been logged and the crowd cheered the big pitcher as he walked back to his dugout.

With two out in the second inning Dick Dietz singled, but Drysdale then got Hal Lanier to ground out on a sinker-ball. With two out in the third Davenport reached base on an error, but Don brushed Mays back, teased him with an outside fast ball, then fed him an inside curve and Willie popped up. With two out in the fourth Dave Marshall singled, but Drysdale threw an inside pitch to Dietz, then struck him out on three straight outside pitches.

This was a true professional at work. Confident of his control, Drysdale was willing to waste as many as three balls to set up batters. Working them in and out, up and down, he kept them off balance. "Anyone can throw strikes," he said, "but forget fat strikes. You can only afford to give the batters one inch of the plate. A half-inch is better."

The Dodgers got Don two runs. Lanier opened the Giants' fifth by ripping a single off the shortstop's glove. Pitcher Mike McCormick bunted him to second. A pick-off attempt was signalled and Drysdale whirled and threw to second, but shortstop Zoilo Versalles had missed the sign and the ball sailed over the unguarded base. The runner sped to third. The crowd tensed with a run only 90 feet from home, but Drysdale set up Davenport with outside pitches, then fed him an inside pitch. Davenport fell back from it, swinging, and popped it up to end the inning.

Mays opened the sixth with a single, but Drysdale got the next three in a row. He then got the Giants one-two-three in both the seventh and eighth innings. Meanwhile the Dodgers got him a third run. As he took the mound for the ninth, he was under enormous pressure. He walked McCovey. Then Jim Hart singled. As the fans groaned, Drysdale missed with four of five pitches to Jim Marshall to load the bases with none out.

Suddenly the odds were heavily against him. Under normal circumstances, manager Walter Alston might have brought in a relief pitcher. But in this situation, he admitted later, "There was no way I was going to take Don out until that first run was scored off him."

Drysdale threw two balls and two strikes to Dietz, then threw an inside pitch. Dietz threw up his left arm and the pitch hit it. This would have forced in a run, except that umpire Harry Wendelsted immediately ruled that the batter had made no effort to avoid the pitch, so it became only "ball three." Dietz and the Giants were furious. They appealed to the umpire, but the decision stood. Dietz returned to bat and hit a fly that was too short for the runner on third to score on.

Pinch-hitter Ty Cline then chopped a grounder to first baseman Wes Parker. To save the run, the play would have to be at home. The runner raced for home and Drysdale ran in to help on the play. Parker threw and the ball headed straight for Drysdale's head. Don saw it and hit the ground just in time. The throw thudded into catcher Jeff Torborg's glove just ahead of the runner for a force-out.

With two out pinch-hitter Jack Hiatt hit a pop fly to Parker. Later Parker remembered thinking, "If I miss it, I'm going to walk off the field and never come back." But he caught it, giving Drysdale his record-tying shutout.

In the dressing room newsmen surrounded him. He stood in front of his locker bathed in hot, bright television lights. "The tension got worse as the game went on," Don admitted. A writer reminded him that he still needed one more shutout to set a new record. If he succeeded at that, he would be within two innings of the major league record for consecutive scoreless innings. "Did you have to tell me?" Don grimaced, and everyone laughed.

The writers and broadcasters stayed for an hour. "I'm exhausted," he admitted. His curly hair was damp and mussed. His handsome face was flushed. It seemed a struggle for him simply to undress. He still had to shower, soak his arm in a tub of ice and dress again. It was after midnight when he walked slowly through the nearly-deserted ballpark out to the dark parking lot to meet his wife and drive home.

The next day he stood in the clubhouse listening to a repeat radio broadcast of the previous night's ninth inning. He paced around nervously. At one point, as though he did not know the outcome, he said, "Get the ball over, you idiot." When the 21-minute inning was over, Don had his head in his hands and he seemed near tears. "I couldn't go through that again," he sighed. "It was just too much."

Soon the pressure began to mount again. The telephone kept ringing. The congratulations and questions kept coming. It was Tuesday, June 4th, the night of a presidential primary election in California, when Don took the mound again, this time to face the Pittsburgh Pirates.

The Dodgers scored three runs early and Drysdale did not give up a hit until Donn Clendenon grounded a single to open the fourth. A moment later Clendenon was out on a double play. With one out in the fifth Gary Kolb hit a double, then reached third on an infield out. But Drysdale then got Maury Wills to ground out, ending the inning. By now the excitement was electric. The big pitcher was throwing powerfully.

He reached the ninth with a 5-0 lead. He struck out Manny Jimenez. One out. He got Matty Alou to bounce to second. Two out. Wills singled to left. Then up came Willie Stargell, the league's hottest hitter. He hit a bouncer to the infield and Drysdale had his sixth shutout in a row. He had pitched 54 consecutive scoreless innings. Walter Johnson, the Hall of Fame pitcher for Washington, had pitched 56 scoreless innings in 1913. Drysdale needed six more outs to tie the record and seven to break it.

At the Ambassador Hotel in downtown Los Angeles later that night, Robert F. Kennedy, who had won the primary election, took a moment in his victory speech to congratulate Drysdale on his remarkable record. By the time Don had showered and changed and walked with his wife to his car in the stadium parking lot, youngsters standing there told him Kennedy had been shot.

His marvelous moment destroyed, Don forgot

After Drysdale (#53) completes his sixth straight shutout, Dodgers come from all directions to congratulate him.

about baseball and stayed up most of the night, as did many others in the country, to keep track of the fallen politician's condition. The vigil endured through the next day into the following morning. Early on Thursday, June 6th, Robert Kennedy died. The next day Bill Ford, who had coached Drysdale in high school, died. Both deaths shook Drysdale, but the world and baseball had to go on.

On Saturday Drysdale watched Kennedy's funeral ceremonies on television. That night he went to the ballpark to face Philadelphia. His face seemed drawn, his manner solemn. As he pitched, the crowd cheered every strike and booed every ball.

The Dodger ace walked one in the first, but the inning ended without a score. In the second Bill White and Tony Taylor grounded out. Don went to 3-and-2 on Clay Dalrymple, then struck him out to tie Walter Johnson's record.

As he walked off, the crowd gave him a thundering ovation. The only fan who was not applauding was his wife, who sat still in her seat, her fingers crossed for good luck. She knew he still needed one more out to break the record.

Roberto Pena opened the third inning. Don threw a fast strike, then a breaking strike. Pena grounded a foul. Don missed outside for ball one. Pena lined a foul. Then he topped a grounder to third. Ken Boyer threw to first for the out. Drysdale stood on tip-toes, smiling broadly and breathing deeply with relief. The fans stood, applauding, whistling and cheering. The last of the records he had sought was his.

Don's streak of scoreless innings continued until the fifth inning when two singles and a fly ball brought a run home—the first run he had allowed in 58 2/3 consecutive innings. After 25 days of steadily mounting tension, the long streak was over.

Donald Scott Drysdale was born on July 23rd, 1936, in Van Nuys, California. His father Scott, a former minor-league player, had retired from the game in the mid 1930s to go to work for the telephone company in Los Angeles. Don was already practicing as a pitcher when he was five years old. Don's mother sometimes played catcher for her son until his fast ball became too hot for her to handle. Even his grandmother helped out. She delivered the papers on his neighborhood newspaper route on days when he had games to play.

To protect his son's arm, however, Don's father insisted he play other positions besides pitcher until he matured. Don became an outstanding infielder and a powerful hitter. Even as a pitcher in the majors, he was a good enough hitter to bat .300 one year. In his years with the Dodgers he hit 29 home runs and batted in 110 runs. Don was a second baseman until his senior year in high school. Then he began to concentrate on his pitching, using the sidearm delivery he had developed.

Drysdale was only 17 years old when he signed a contract with the Brooklyn Dodgers in June of 1954. He had an 8-5 record for Bakersfield in the California League in 1954 and achieved an 11-11 mark for

Montreal in the International League in 1955. He was promoted to the majors in 1956, before he had passed his 20th birthday. In his first season with Brooklyn he won five and lost five, but in his second season he was the team's biggest winner at 17-9.

After the 1956 season the Dodgers moved from Brooklyn to Los Angeles. In his first four seasons in Los Angeles Drysdale had won-and-lost records of 12-13, 17-13, 15-14 and 13-10. Everyone agreed that the lanky youngster had a delivery that was difficult for batters to follow, exceptional speed, great breaking pitches and good control. No one understood why he did not do better.

There were many reasons. For one thing, Don had a terrible temper. He often got so angry at himself during a game that he came apart emotionally and lost his concentration. After one game in which he had lost a big lead, he stormed into the clubhouse and threw everything in his locker on the floor. Then he took off his glove, cap, jacket and shirt and threw them on the floor. He saw a bat bag and kicked it. Loaded with bats, it hurt his foot, making him even angrier. He kicked it again, then picked it up and tried to throw it across the room. His spikes slipped on the floor and he fell heavily. The bats rolled in all directions. Finally he rounded up the bats, stuffed them back in the bag, hauled it to the door and threw it out. Only then was his tantrum over and all his angry energy spent.

Throwing close to batters also involved Don in many controversies. He led the National League in

Standing high on the mound, Drysdale goes through his elaborate pitching motion.

hit batters several seasons. During one season he hit 20 batters, more than most pitchers hit in their careers. Eddie Matthews, Vada Pinson, Frank Robinson and Willie Mays are among the players who threatened or threw punches at Drysdale over the years. Drysdale was fined or suspended a number of times. He would only say, "I pitch tight. It's my bread and butter." He also was accused of throwing a spit-ball, which is illegal. "My mother always told me never to put my dirty fingers in my mouth," he laughed.

Drysdale's temper was understandable to a point, however. It was not easy pitching for the Dodgers in those years. During their first years in Los Angeles they played in a football field, the Coliseum, which had a 250-foot left-field wall. Drysdale detested it, considering it unfair. "The batter hits the ball on his knuckles and, ping, it's in the left-field seats," he complained. Even more discouraging, the Dodgers seldom got him runs. One year they scored only 15 runs for him in the 16 games he lost.

Gradually, however, he matured. In 1962 the Dodgers moved into spacious Dodger Stadium, making a pop-fly home run a thing of the past. In the first year in the new stadium Don put together a 25-9 record with a 2.84 earned run average. He led the league with 232 strikeouts and won the Cy Young award. He still had to struggle for precious victories. He was 19-17 in 1963 and 18-16 in 1964, although he had a lower earned run average each year. He then went 23-12 in 1965

Explaining his improvement, Drysdale commented, "I'm a perfectionist. I hate making mistakes. I can't stand to lose. But I had to learn to take the bad with the good before I could become a good pitcher. It was a long while, however, before I realized how much I was hurting myself by getting mad at myself. Eventually I realized I had to just give it everything I had every game and then forget about it, win or lose, and go on to the next one. Only then did I become a consistently effective pitcher game after game, season after season."

All these years "The Big D" was something of an "iron man." He often led the league in games started, complete games and innings pitched. He missed only three starts in ten seasons. He might limp home to his wife Ginger and daughter Kelly as lame as the lamest horse on his suburban ranch, but he was always back and ready to go the next game. If he did miss a start with an injury, he made sure he did not miss the next one. Once he missed a start with a broken thumb, then ripped off the splint so he could pitch in turn the next time.

Rival manager Gene Mauch once said, "If I had my choice of any pitcher in baseball, I'd take Drysdale because he's so dependable—a true professional." Don's own manager, Walter Alston, said, "Every four days, Don is ready to work nine innings, week after week, month after month, year after year. You never have to worry about him."

Drysdale thrived on challenge. He pitched in eight All-Star games and did not give up an earned run in the last six of them. He pitched in four World Series and sometimes was spectacular. In the 1959 World Series against Chicago, Don pitched a 3-1 triumph. In the Dodgers' 1963 four-game sweep of New York, Don beat Jim Bouton and the Yankees on a three-hitter, 1-0. Knocked out in the first game against Minnesota in 1965, Drysdale came back to win the fourth game, 7-2, on a five-hitter. He was ready to pitch the seventh game, but was passed over in favor of Sandy Koufax.

Throughout his L.A. career Drysdale worked in the shadow of the less reliable but more spectacular Koufax and he was denied much credit that might have been due him had he pitched for another team. But he never complained and gave Koufax high credit, calling him one of the greatest pitchers in baseball history.

In 1966 and 1967 the aging Drysdale labored to 13-16 records. In 1968, despite his spectacular shutout streak, he wound up with a 14-12 mark. Because of his especially elaborate and excessive pitching motion, baseball observers warned that he would ruin his arm soemday. It finally happened, but only after Don had pitched 14 seasons in the majors. The stress of his long career eventually tore and virtually destroyed the muscles in his right shoulder.

He suffered through most of 1969, winning five games and losing four, before he finally retired. He had just turned 33 and was only one year past his great streak of shutout pitching, but he had become ineffective and every pitch caused him terrible pain.

An unhappy Drysdale announces his retirement in 1969.

At a press conference called to announce his retirement, he fought back tears and said, "All of my boyhood dreams have come true. I wouldn't trade a minute of the time I've had in baseball. But there are three things that are inevitable—death, taxes and the retirement of a professional athlete."

When Sandy Koufax had retired, Drysdale had said, "Sandy was a great one. But cruel as it is to say, he's gone now and baseball goes on. I'm still here, but when I'm gone the game will go on without me, too." Like Koufax, Drysdale was forced to retire early. And although the game went on, Drysdale's records and the memories of his great achievements would not be quickly forgotten.

6. JIM BUNNING

THEIR NAMES WERE Barbara, Jimmy, Joan, Cathy, Bill, Bridget, Mark, Dave and Amy. There were nine of them, including two sets of twins, and they were Jim Bunning's children. Jim was the champion father of the major leagues in the 1960s, so it was appropriate that his greatest day in the big leagues came on a Father's Day.

On Sunday, June 21st, 1964, Jim was pitching for the Philadelphia Phillies in Shea Stadium, New York, against the New York Mets. After four innings he realized that he had retired 12 men in a row. Opening the fifth, Bunning got the Mets' Joe Christopher to pop up. Then Jesse Gonder stepped in. On the second pitch he smashed a low liner toward right field. "I had thrown a change-up and got it too fat, right over the plate. I thought it was a hit," Jim said later.

But second baseman Tony Taylor took a couple of steps toward first base and dove, reaching out with his glove hand. The ball landed squarely in the pocket of his glove but jarred loose when Taylor hit the ground. The little Cuban scrambled for the loose ball, picked it up, twisted around while still on his knees and threw to first base just ahead of Gonder. "I never thought I had a chance, but I knew I had to try," Taylor admitted later.

"When he made that great play, I knew I had something special going," Bunning recalled afterwards. He got the next batter to ground out. When he got three more in the sixth inning, he had retired 18 men in a row.

By now the crowd realized that Bunning had a chance at that rarest of pitching performances, a "perfect game," in which no rival batter reaches base by any means. Among the crowd were Jim's wife Mary and his eldest daughter, 12-year-old Barbara, who had come from the Bunning's home in Fort Thomas, Kentucky, to visit the World's Fair. "That's my daddy," she kept saying to the fans around her.

The pressure was heavy not only on Bunning, but on all of the Phillies because anything resembling a mistake—an error, for example—would spoil the perfect game. No pitcher had won a perfect game in regular-season play since 1922. Don Larsen of the Yankees had pitched a perfect game in the 1956 World Series against the Brooklyn Dodgers, and Harvey Haddix of Pittsburgh had pitched 12 perfect innings against the Milwaukee Braves in 1959 but had lost the game in the 13th inning. If he could complete the game without allowing a baserunner, Bunning would become the first National Leaguer

Jim Bunning pitches to the New York Mets during his no-hitter in June of 1964.

and the fourth major leaguer to win such a game during the regular season.

Although there is a baseball superstition against mentioning a no-hitter while the game is still in progress, Bunning talked about his between innings from the time he realized he had a chance. "I figured it would make it easier to live with it if I lost it," he smiled later. When he came back to the dugout after the sixth inning, he said, "Nine more outs to go, fellows." His teammates were shocked. "Dive if you have to," he added, remembering Taylor's diving stop. In the seventh inning Jim Hickman struck out, Ron Hunt grounded out and Ed Kranepool struck out. "Six more outs to go," Bunning said as he sat down in the dugout.

The fans in Shea Stadium had divided loyalties. They wanted their Mets to win, but they also were friendly to Bunning. They reacted on every one of his pitches, making lots of noise. By the eighth inning the Phils led, 6-0, and the tall, slender, curveballing sidearmer was the center of attention. In the Mets' eighth Joe Christopher struck out and Jesse Gonder grounded out. Then Bob Taylor was called out on strikes, but the Phils' catcher Gus Triandos dropped the ball. Taylor ran for first as Triandos hurriedly scooped up the loose ball and fired it to first. Taylor was out and the perfect game was still safe. "Three more outs," Bunning said as he reached the dugout. "Dive, jump, do anything you have to do." His teammates nodded tensely.

Bunning had perfect control that day, seldom throwing two balls in a row to any batter. Only twice did he throw three balls to a batter. He was not having to throw many pitches and he was working fast. But he confessed later, "It seemed to take forever. I knew what I had going for me and I didn't think I'd ever get it. The ninth inning seemed to last an eternity."

Catcher Triandos said later, "Before the ninth he said to me, 'I'd sure like to borrow Sandy Koufax's fast ball for this last inning.' I said, 'Your fast ball and your breaking balls are plenty good enough.' But he was chattering like a little boy. From nerves, I guess."

In the Mets' ninth Charlie Smith led off. He fouled off the first pitch. He took a high inside pitch for ball one. Then he swung and popped a high foul which Triandos chased to the stands back of home plate, but which landed on the screen. Smith took an outside pitch for ball two, then swung at a slider and hit a high foul off the third-base line, just beyond the base, which shortstop Bobby Wine caught. Two outs to go. Bunning was throwing mostly curves and sliders now. Pinch-hitter George Altman came up next. He fouled a curve ball down the right-field line for strike one. Then Bunning threw a slider and Altman fouled it back for strike two. Jim threw another slider and the slugger swung and missed for the second out. There was only one out left and the Met fans were now on Bunning's side. They were on their feet cheering him on.

Bunning summoned catcher Triandos to the mound for a conference. Unsure what he wanted, Triandos hurried out to his pitcher. "Tell me a joke or something. I have to relax," Bunning said. Triandos could only laugh and shake his head and pat his pitcher on the back. He returned nervously to his position behind the plate. Pinch-hitter John Stephenson stepped in. Bunning threw him a curve and he swung and missed. Bunning threw him a slider, which Stephenson took, but which cut the corner of the plate for strike two. Then Bunning missed the plate with a fast ball and a curve. Bunning turned his back on the batter for a moment. Then he returned to his stance and threw a curve. Stephenson swung and missed.

Bunning pounded his glove with his fist in joy. Triandos rushed the ball out to him as he was mobbed by his teammates. The crowd stood and cheered. Jim's wife and daughter were crying with excitement and pleasure.

Six years earlier Jim had pitched his first no-hitter (but not a perfect game) for the Detroit Tigers. His second no-hitter made him the first pitcher since the legendary Cy Young to pitch a no-hitter in both major leagues.

A most unusual and long-lasting pitcher, James Paul David Bunning was born October 23rd, 1931, at Southgate, Kentucky, just across the Ohio River from Cincinnati. His father worked for a ladder company but loved sports and encouraged Jim to participate in them. Jim grew up to be tall and slim, especially good at both baseball and basketball. At 18, he accepted a basketball scholarship to Xavier University in Ohio, but soon afterward he signed a professional baseball contract with Detroit for $4,500.

He grew to a height of 6-foot-3 and a weight of 200 pounds. Although he could throw hard, he did not have an overpowering fast ball. He had to develop good breaking pitches and good control to take advantage of his talent. For six long seasons he bounced around the minor leagues learning his trade. He played at Richmond, Indiana, of the Ohio-Indiana League; Davenport, Iowa, of the Three-I League; Williamsport, Pennsylvania, of the Eastern League; Buffalo, New York, of the International League; and Little Rock, Arkansas, of the Southern League, winning 41 games and losing 55 in those difficult years.

Not all star pitchers become stars overnight. Times were hard for Jim Bunning for a long time. He got married after three years in the minors and as his family grew, he found it difficult to make ends meet. He coached freshman basketball at Xavier two winters for extra money. He also went to college classes in the off-season until he graduated with a degree in economics in 1953. "Nothing was going to stop me from getting that degree," he has explained. "Some say I would have made the majors sooner if I had concentrated on it sooner, but I felt getting a college education was as important to me as getting a fast start in baseball, and I feel now I just developed later than most players."

He had a quick temper he had to learn to control. When he lost many games early in his career, he grew frustrated and angry. He recalled that in the minors he sometimes refused to give up the ball when the manager came to the mound to take him out of a game. "I was always mad," he remembers. At the same time he was learning to control his temper, he was struggling to control his curve ball. Still, Detroit officials had confidence he would find himself sooner or later. They considered him a pitcher with high potential despite his losing record in the minors. They brought him up to the majors for part of the 1955 season. He appeared in 15 games for Detroit, winning three and losing five.

He divided 1956 between Charleston, West Virginia, of the American Association, where he struggled to a 9-11 mark, and Detroit, where he won five of six decisions. During the off-season he accepted an offer to pitch winter baseball in Cuba. There he concentrated on developing his slider. He threw sliders three pitches out of four. He got to be very good with it. With his regular curve, his good fast ball and his improving control, he finally was ready. In 1957 he was in the majors to stay, putting together a surprising and sensational first full season in the big time, winning 20 and losing only eight. He led the league with 267 innings pitched and compiled a fine 2.70 earned run average.

From that point Jim was a fine professional pitcher. He often played for losing teams that gave him little scoring support, but he was strong and consistent, starting 35 to 40 games and pitching 250 to 300 innings every year for more than a decade. He had won-and-lost records of 14-12, 17-13, 11-14, 17-11, 19-10 and 12-13 for Detroit. After the 1963 season the Tigers traded him out of the American League to Philadelphia in the National League. Here he gained season records of 19-8, 19-9, 19-14, and

Bunning pitches for Detroit. He won 118 games for them before being traded to the National League.

17-15. The 20-game total is the one at which pitchers aim each season and it was disappointing to Jim to fall only one short four different times.

He pitched for only two top teams, the 1961 Tigers, who finished second in the American League, and the 1964 Phillies, who seemed to be on their way to the pennant before they collapsed in the last few weeks of the season. Bunning called the failure of the Phillies his "greatest single disappointment." He had always hoped to start and win the first World Series game some year but was denied his dream. His experience in 1967 was another disappointment. His record was an unremarkable 17-15, but it failed to tell the whole story. In 11 of the games he lost, the Phils scored a grand total of five runs. He lost five separate games by 1-0, a National League record.

One early evening before a night game, Bunning sat in the dugout as the fans began to drift toward their seats in the big stadium. "It is very difficult to go out and work nine good innings, two to three hours, and get nothing out of it game after game," he said. "But if you're a major leaguer, you just have to accept it and learn to keep on going out there and giving your best. You hope the breaks will even out over a period of years, but in some cases perhaps they don't."

"However, I've had more than my share of success. I have no complaints," he continued. On the field the players were loosening up, going through their pre-game practice routines in a carefree way. The sound of bat against ball and the laughter of grown men drifted across the diamond. "There are worse ways to make a living," the veteran concluded.

With a wife and nine children to support, Bunning had become one of the modern businessmen athletes, selling securities successfully during the off-season. He was a quiet, self-assured person, who conducted himself in a very businesslike way. He was a good negotiator with his teams and generally received the salary he asked for because he knew what he was worth. He became one of the highest paid pitchers in baseball, though not as well-known as a Don Drysdale or a Tom Seaver.

Although the season did not end until the first of October each year, Bunning began preparing for the next season about the first of November. He went to the YMCA and ran on a regular basis. He liked to fish, hunt and play golf. Golf was especially important because it involved a lot of walking and kept his legs in shape.

He led a lonely life during the season because his family was too large to be moved around with him. On-season and off-season, he watched his diet and kept in perfect shape. Managers referred to him as a perfect professional who was always ready to give his best. He took baseball seriously and his seriousness enabled him to last longer in it than most players.

One year during spring training he arrived earlier than the other regulars and was found pitching batting practice to rookies. This surprised a writer, who asked him why he was doing it.

"I need the work to get ready," Bunning said.

"Others wouldn't do it," the writer commented.

"I'm not others," he replied. "It took me a long time to learn how to pitch the way I have to pitch, and the reason I work hard is that I like it in the majors and want to stay as long as I can.

"If there is a secret to my success beyond hard work, it is that I am one of those pitchers who can recognize early in a game what my best pitch is on that given day or night and can concentrate on that," he once said. "You don't throw it all the time, but you try to set up the batters for it. Even if it is a pitch the batter happens to hit best, you still pitch it because you have to go to your strength even if it means matching your strength against his strength."

Bunning had a sort of awkward motion that fell somewhere between three-quarter-arm and sidearm. His great strength was his control. "Concentration and control are the keys" he said. "You have to concentrate. I've always tried to have an idea of what I want to do with each pitch. Control is most important because without that you can't do anything with your pitches."

Former Phils' manager Gene Mauch once said, "He operates like a fine surgeon. He makes a tiny incision here, then another there."

If Bunning had a weakness as a pitcher, it was a tendency to throw home-run balls. He led the American League in most home runs allowed with 37 in 1959 and 38 in 1963. However, as time passed, he reduced this problem, and his earned run averages,

Bunning falls toward first base after a pitch but keeps his eye on the ball. Second base is in the background.

which were higher than most top pitchers for a number of years, began to decline late in his career. He led the National League in shutouts with five in 1966 and six in 1967.

Bunning tied for the National League lead in hit batsmen with 12 in 1965 and led with 19 in 1966 and 13 in 1967. Like Don Drysdale he was not afraid to brush batters back and this touched off a number of rhubarbs. At various times in Bunning's career Jim Piersall charged him from home plate, Mickey Mantle threatened to do so and Minnie Minoso threw a bat at him. "Show me a good pitcher who doesn't throw at hitters and I'll show you ten who do," he once said angrily. However, he has explained, "I came by my tactic honestly. My style was to pitch low-and-away and I'd try to move the batters back from the plate by pitching high and in close on my early deliveries."

Bunning was accused of cutting baseballs with his belt-buckle to provide a rough surface to grip and rubbing baseballs with pine-tar or spit to provide a smooth surface from which his pitches might slip. In either case a pitcher might be able to make the ball "do tricks" which it might not do under legal conditions. However, most top pitchers are subjected to such accusations because their pitches are harder to hit than those of ordinary hurlers. Bunning has been a tough, competitive craftsman who has learned a wide variety of pitches and made them work for him.

Although Jim never had the opportunity to challenge a World Series foe, he was selected to pitch in eight All-Star games. In seven of them he did not give up a single earned run. In 1961, when the leagues were playing two All-Star games each season, Jim pitched in both and worked five hitless, runless frames, providing one of the great individual performances in the history of this classic.

Despite the care he took of himself, including that of packing his arm in ice-bags for an hour after each start, the hard-working Bunning developed arm trouble in the late 1960s. He seemed to be on his way out of baseball several times. Philadelphia traded him to Pittsburgh for 1968. He had only a 4-14 mark for the Pirates and they traded him to Los Angeles in the middle of the 1969 season. He finished the year with a 13-10 record. The Dodgers released him after the season to make room for younger players, but the Phillies signed him again for 1970.

Bunning struggled to a record of ten victories and 15 defeats, giving him a lifetime record of 219-172. He also had 2,796 strikeouts, the third-best total in major league history, surpassed only by Walter Johnson's 3,499 and Cy Young's 2,803. He needed only eight more strikeouts to pass Young in the standings.

His next-to-last victory in 1970 was his 100th in the National League to go with his 118 American League victories. He was only the second pitcher ever to win 100 games in both leagues and received wide publicity for this accomplishment.

"Being the first pitcher since Cy Young to win 100 or more games in each league is a freak thing," he commented. "It's just a matter of being traded from league to league in the middle of your career. However, winning 200 or more games anywhere is an accomplishment I'm proud of."

Thirty-nine years of age shortly after the 1970 season ended, Bunning was thinking about retirement. As the breadwinner for nine children, he had resisted retirement in prior campaigns. "You're only as old as you feel," he said. "Some athletes are old at 28. Some take care of themselves and are young at 38. There comes a time when any professional athlete must quit, but those of us who really love sports hang on as long as we can produce." He looked across the field on which players were practicing. Every one of them was younger than he, who had played in the major leagues for 16 seasons. "It is a struggle to get here and often painful to stay here. But you don't leave easily," he said.

7. HOYT WILHELM

OPPOSING BATTERS called it "The Moth" or "The Butterfly." They had been trying to hit it for nearly 30 years with little success. Catchers called it "The Thing" and the glove they tried to catch it with they called "The Monster." They failed to catch it with embarrassing frequency.

It, of course, was Hoyt Wilhelm's knuckleball, the most baffling pitch in baseball. Like most knuckleballs, it was misnamed. Different pitchers who throw the knuckleball hold it differently, but few place their knuckles on the ball. Wilhelm cradled his between the tips of his index and middle finger and his thumb and applied pressure to the ball with his fingertips as he released it. The ball would leave his hand with little or no spin. For the first 55 feet or so it seemed to float. Then in the last few feet, just before it passed the batter, it dipped or darted this way or that.

"I have no idea what it is going to do or exactly where it is going to go," Wilhelm admitted. "I throw

Hoyt Wilhelm demonstrates his grip on his "knuckleball" after being traded to the Chicago Cubs in September 1970.

it at different speeds and it does something different every time. This is why it is so difficult for catchers to handle and batters to judge. My success comes because the one thing I can do with it is keep it over the plate."

Wilhelm once went to the Aberdeen Proving Grounds in Maryland and threw the knuckleball in a wind tunnel. Technicians set up electronic cameras and intricate machinery so they could measure it. He threw it for a half-hour and they gave up. They said they could test bullets and scale models of rockets which could be programmed precisely to go to the moon, but they had no idea why the knuckleball did what it did or when it was going to do it.

There have been other knuckleball pitchers. In fact Hoyt got the idea for his knuckler from reading about Emil "Dutch" Leonard, who pitched in the American League in the late 1930s and early 1940s. At one time Washington had four knuckleball starters, including Leonard. "I fell in love with the pitch, reading about it," Wilhelm once recalled.

He learned to throw the knuckler as a boy, practicing and mastering it mostly on his own. As a farmboy in Cornelius, North Carolina, he had plenty of room to practice in, and if he was wild, no windows would be broken. He used the knuckler on the sandlots and in high school ball and from the beginning of his professional career in 1942.

Most pitchers try to learn how to throw the knuckleball late in their careers as an "extra pitch," which may make them effective for a few extra seasons. In recent years Phil Niekro has won big with a knuckler. But no one could match Wilhelm's success with it.

Most reliefers are fast-ball pitchers who fire their big pitch past tired batters in the late innings.

Many of them fade after a few seasons when their arms give out. Wilhelm was primarily a relief pitcher throughout his major league career. Although he was successful as a starter and once pitched a no-hitter, he became the most durable and perhaps the greatest relief pitcher of all time. He held all the important records available to these specialists. By the end of the 1970 season he had 124 victories and 223 saves for a total of 347. He had appeared in 990 games as a reliefer, striking out 1,334 men in 1,825 innings. He gained another all-time record by appearing in 1,042 games as a starter or in relief.

"If I had been a fast-ball pitcher or a starter, I could not possibly have lasted as long as I have," Wilhelm once said. As the 1970s began he had been pitching professionally for 29 years and had been in the major leagues for 19 years. He had been passed around among nine different major league teams as each in turn felt he was growing too old to be useful. But at the age of 47 he still was performing brilliantly. Ty Cobb hit .357 at the age of 40. Warren Spahn pitched 23 victories at the age of 40. But at 47 Hoyt Wilhelm was still winning games and saving games regularly with his remarkable knuckleball. He stood as one of the marvels of the sport.

Wilhelm, born July 26th, 1923, graduated from Cornelius High School in 1942 and started pitching with Mooresville, North Carolina, of the Carolina League, 35 miles from his home town. "I was 18 years old," he recalled. "I signed for a salary of $85 a month and it was great. There were no bonuses in those days. But you will never hear me complain I was born 20 years too soon. Baseball has been good to me."

Wilhelm had a 10-3 record for Mooresville. Then World War II interrupted his career. Hoyt was drafted into the Army and served for three years. He became a staff sergeant with the 99th Infantry, fought and was wounded, winning the Purple Heart in the Battle of the Bulge in Europe.

With the war won and a discharge in his hands, Wilhelm returned to baseball and Mooresville. At this point came the lone occasion when Wilhelm considered giving up his knuckler. He has recalled, "The manager at Moorseville was an old-timer named Ginger Watts and he had the same idea most everybody else had then—that the knuckleball was something you developed only after you lost your fastball. He told me I had to change or I'd never get anywhere in baseball. I tried switching to curves and fastballs like other pitchers, and I got my brains knocked out. So I went back to the knuckleball and Ginger never brought it up again."

His brief experiment with standard pitching equipment ended, Wilhelm went on to 21-8 and 20-7 records as a starter for Mooresville. He was a starter in 1948 and 1949 for Jacksonville in the South Atlantic League and Knoxville in the Tri-State League, recording 13-9 and 17-12 marks. In 1950 and 1951 he started for Minneapolis in the American Association, recording 15-11 and 11-14 marks. But no one had faith in a pure knuckleballer, and ten long years after he had turned professional, Wilhelm still had not pitched in the major leagues.

His chance came the following spring. Leo Durocher, then managing the New York Giants, invited Wilhelm to pre-season camp for a trial in 1952. At first look, the skipper was unimpressed. "I don't know," he said to his veteran infielder, Bill Rigney, "his ball doesn't do much. What do you think?"

"I'd like to see how he does in a game," said Rigney.

"Warm him up," said Durocher, "and we'll see."

Rigney picked up a catcher's mitt and walked to the bullpen to work with the 28-year-old rookie. The first pitch glanced off the bottom of his mitt. The second hit him on the shins. The third grazed his leg.

"I knew then," Rigney recalls, "that Hoyt Wilhelm was just a little above the ordinary."

Rigney suggested to Durocher that if the fellow's pitches were hard to catch, batters might find them hard to hit. Durocher could not see him as a regular starter, however. He needed help in his bullpen and decided to try the newcomer as a relief pitcher. He figured that if they saw it an inning or two at a time, batters would never catch up to the knuckler. He was right.

That season Wilhelm appeared in more games, 71, than any pitcher in the National League. He also led in winning percentage with .833, based on 15 wins and only three losses, and he had the best

Wilhelm, then a 29-year-old rookie with the New York Giants, winds up to pitch. Eighteen years later he was still pitching.

earned run average, 2.43. He was the first rookie ever to lead the circuit in both winning percentage and earned run average. Wilhelm saved 11 games, helped the Giants into second place and placed second in the Rookie of the Year voting to Joe Black, a relief pitcher who helped the Brooklyn Dodgers to the pennant with similar relief statistics.

"I had never pitched relief before, but I was a relief pitcher from then on for most of my career," Wilhelm said later. "If I had been just fair in relief, maybe I'd have been a starting pitcher and everything would have been different all these years. I might have just lasted a couple of years and then again maybe I'd still be pitching up here as a starter. This is something no one can possibly know."

From 1953 to 1956 Wilhelm worked in from 55 to 70 games each season, won 27 and saved 30 for the New Yorkers. In 1954 he helped the Giants to the pennant with a 12-4 record and pitched scoreless innings in each of two World Series games. However, after he slipped to 4-9 in 1956, the Giants gave up on him. He was 33 years old and seemed to be on the decline. If they had kept him then, they could have had perhaps fifteen years of valuable pitching from him. But they traded him to the St. Louis Cardinals for the 1957 season.

Wilhelm seemed shaken by the move and could not get going in St. Louis. He won only one of five decisions with them and was released to the Cleveland Indians in the American League on waivers. He went 0-1 with Cleveland the last part of that season.

In 1958 he worked both as a starter and in relief and went 2-7 for the Indians before they waived him to Baltimore near the end of that campaign. In Baltimore, manager Paul Richards, considered a wonder with pitchers, worked with Wilhelm and is credited with helping him regain his rhythm.

He went only 1-3 for Baltimore the last part of the 1958 campaign, but the one was a big one. On September 20th he started against New York, only his ninth major league start, and pitched a no-hitter against the Yankees. When the Yankees' Hank Bauer flied out to end the game, the stunned crowd came to its feet to cheer the surprising showing of the 35-year-old veteran. "It's sort of unbelievable," a dazed Wilhelm whispered later in the madness of the dressing room.

In May of the following season Wilhelm pitched a one-hitter against the same Yankee club. He started 27 games in 1959, finished 13, won 15, lost 11 and had a 2.19 earned run average for the Orioles. His ERA led the American League and made Wilhelm the only hurler in history to lead both leagues in this department.

Wilhelm, a solid fielder, held the major league record for pitchers by having gone 319 consecutive games without making an error. He was not so kind to his catchers. While he was pitching for Baltimore, his catchers tied the league record of four passed balls in a game six times and tied the record of three passed balls in an inning three times.

Desperate, manager Richards devised an oversized catcher's mitt which measured 42 inches in circumference (compared to the standard 34 inches) just to catch Wilhelm's knuckler. Later the major leagues limited the size of a catcher's mitt to 38 inches, leaving Wilhelm's catchers out of luck. When Wilhelm joined the White Sox, catcher J. C. Martin set a modern major league record for one season with 33 passed balls in 112 games.

Clearly even a net would have been insufficient to flag down all of "The Knuck's" butterfly pitches. "I feel for my catchers," Wilhelm sighed. "I don't throw so much to spots as I pitch to an area. I get it over the plate a high percentage of the time, but wind resistance seems to make it dart up or drop off or break one way or another all of a sudden. Usually it dances. The big thing is that it has to break every time since I'm not pitching to spots or overpowering anyone. If I lose the feel for it for awhile and it doesn't break, it doesn't do anything and it's murdered. Fortunately this has been rare."

Baltimore had some good young pitchers who were developing as starters, so after his exceptional 1959 season, Wilhelm gradually was eased back into the bullpen. He went 11-8, 9-7 and 7-10 his next three seasons with the Orioles. Then they felt he was starting to slip and traded him to the White Sox for the 1963 season. His first season in Chicago was the last one in which Wilhelm started in any games, though he has threatened to start a game on his 50th birthday.

Wilhelm worked for the White Sox six years, winning 41 games and saving 98. In some respects 1964 was his best year ever. He had a 12-9 record and a 1.99 ERA and set his all-time personal highs with 27 saves and 73 appearances. The latter was the third-best single-season mark in history. Three of the best ten marks for appearances by a pitcher were held by Wilhelm. His ERA kept going down—to 1.81 the next season, 1.67 the next and 1.31 the one after that. His performances in his 40s may be unrivalled in the history of baseball. He worked in 45 or more games every season and was consistently effective.

In his last season in Chicago, 1968, he appeared in 72 games. But he was 45 years old at season's end, and the White Sox could not believe he could go on much longer. He was chosen in the expansion draft by the new Kansas City Royals, but they promptly traded him to the California Angels. The Anaheim club seemed afraid to use him too much. He made only 44 appearances for them in 1969 and won only five of 12 decisions. However, Atlanta, battling for the National League's Eastern Division pennant, was desperate for pitching help and purchased him on September 8th.

In the last three weeks of the season Wilhelm worked in eight games, won two, saved four more and helped save another. The Braves won the pennant and Braves' officials said Wilhelm had won it for them. He had been acquired too late to be eligible for the championship playoff and the Braves lost to the New York Mets. Wilhelm might have saved

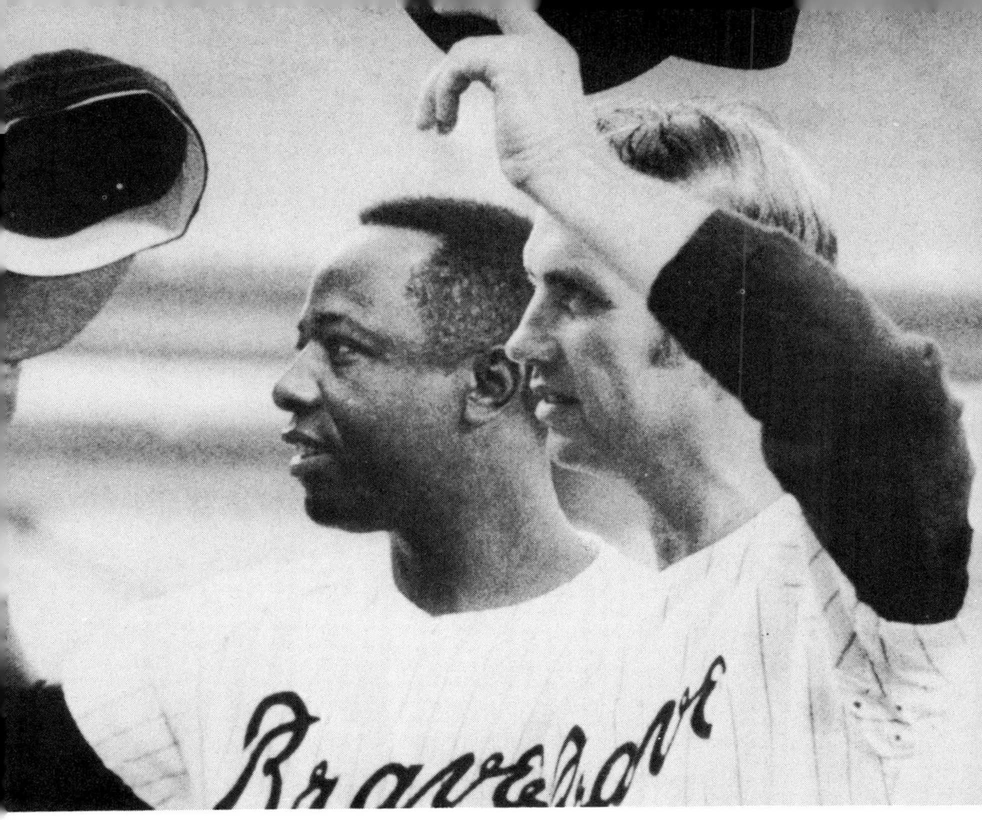

Wilhelm and Hank Aaron, the heroes of the 1969 Atlanta Braves, tip their hats to the crowd.

the playoff too if he had had the chance.

Over the years he had been traded three times, released on waivers twice, released in the expansion draft once and sold once. Nearly everyone thought he would soon collapse. But in September of 1970 he was bought by the Chicago Cubs who were fighting for the pennant. Unfortunately they folded before Wilhelm could take hold. For the year he had 13 saves and six wins. At the end of the season the Cubs sent him back to Atlanta in a trade.

In July of 1968 he pitched in his 907th game to surpass Cy Young's major league record of 906 appearances for a pitcher, which had stood since 1911. In May of 1970, he became the first major league pitcher to appear in 1,000 games. He received a standing ovation, but shrugged it off. "It's only a number," he said. "Why is 1,000 so much more than 998 or 999? It's only a couple more times out there."

By the end of the 1970 season Wilhelm's more than 1,000 appearances represented less than 2,500 innings of work. However, this statistic is deceiving. Some consider it more difficult to pitch an inning or two every game or two than it is to pitch nine innings every fourth or fifth day with plenty of rest in between. A top reliever like Wilhelm had to warm up almost every game and may have pitched two or three innings in the bullpen for every inning he actually pitched in a game.

Wilhelm and his wife, Peggy, had two daughters and a son and lived quietly in the off-season in Columbus, Georgia. He dieted constantly and walked as much as possible. "I hunt and when I don't hunt, I just walk," he said. "As long as the legs hold up, I seem to hold up. I've never had any trouble with my legs. Or with my arm. I throw eight or nine knuckleballs out of every ten pitches, I don't throw too hard and my arm seems to hold up fine."

Wilhelm has been sidelined by an injury only once in his entire career. Practicing bunting against a mechanical pitching machine in 1966, he broke a finger and missed six weeks. Though a physical marvel,

Wilhelm was no slugger. He hit a home run in his first game in the majors and a triple in his second season and had not hit another one of either through 1970. He got his first *hit* in four seasons in a game in 1970 and was so surprised he almost was thrown out at first.

Wilhelm was always a remarkable competitor. Perhaps the most difficult aspect of relief pitching is the pressure. No one expects any pitcher to be on top of his game every time out but a relief pitcher nearly always comes into a game in a critical situation. Usually there are men on bases. Almost any mistake the reliever makes can cost his team a game. A starter can give up a homer and win. The reliever who gives up a homer will often lose.

The quiet, easy-going southerner once said, "It's all in the temperament. You have to do your best and accept things the way they come out. You can't be the kind who blows up emotionally and endure at this relief-pitching business for long."

Ted Williams listed Wilhelm with Whitey Ford, Bob Lemon, Bob Feller and Eddie Lopat as the five toughest pitchers he had ever faced. Hank Aaron, the great Braves' slugger, laughs about the first time he ever faced Wilhelm. "I swung and the ball hit my foot," he recalls.

Jack Quinn, who ended his career in Cincinnati in the 1930's, pitched to the age of 49. This is a standard Wilhelm could surpass, but every year is an added surprise and he could retire at any time.

"Sometimes I feel as though I can pitch until I'm

60," the veteran pitcher has said. There was gray in his hair. A bit of his belly extended over his belt-buckle. Many of his teammates were young enough to be his sons. But Wilhelm was still game. He hoped to complete 30 years in baseball and 20 years in the majors before retiring.

"I feel about the same as I always did, honestly," he sighed. "I've been pitching about as well as I ever did. I don't notice any difference. I'm used to this. This has been my life for a long time now. I'll miss it when I lose it. I don't know what I'll do without it. I reckon I'll go on as long as I can do a job and as long as they'll have me," he said.

8. SAM McDOWELL

SAM McDOWELL was once asked how his fast ball approached the plate. "All of a sudden," Sam replied. "All of a sudden." Ever since, he has had the nickname "Sudden," or "Sudden Sam." Sometimes he was also called "Pepper" because before a game he could play "pepper" by the hour. Pepper is a warm-up drill in which one man tosses the ball to a batter, fields the batter's choppy grounder, and swiftly lobs it back to the batter. "Pepper" McDowell had a lot of nervous energy to wear off.

McDowell was one of the more spectacular pitchers since Sandy Koufax. But he was also a player who disappointed fans and writers because he never quite lived up to his potential. In the late 1960s he struck out batters at a faster rate than any other hurler in history, but he frequently had trouble winning as many games as he lost. Although he first appeared in the majors in 1962, it was 1970 before he won 20 games in one season. Most of this time he pitched for teams that provided him little scoring

Sam McDowell, a 17-year-old high school pitching star (left), after he signed with the Cleveland Indians in 1960. At right, Sam appears during 1970 as a veteran Indian pitcher.

support. But Sam himself was erratic. Although his fast ball was explosive, he was wild and he seemed to fold in tough situations.

The 6-foot-6 210-pounder was a left-hander. As fans watched him struggle through the 1960s, they were reminded that left-handed pitchers—Sandy Koufax, Lefty Grove and Carl Hubbell—did not mature until late in their careers. But McDowell seemed to lack confidence in himself. "Did you ever stop to think Sam McDowell may not be a super-pitcher?" he asked. "Maybe I'm only a 15-game winner and that's all anyone should expect."

In many ways Sam McDowell seemed uncomfortable in baseball. He had as many interests off the field as he had on the field. He collected and built guns. He was an expert cabinetmaker and a painter of still-lifes. He trained German Shepherd dogs. He often carried painting and woodworking equipment on road-trips with the team and worked at his hobbies in his hotel room.

McDowell was a puzzle to baseball writers since he seemed to tell them anything that popped into his mind. He often made up stories and teased people, refusing to take himself very seriously. He was accused of not taking his baseball too seriously either. He seemed unable to concentrate consistently while pitching and lost many games he should have won. At times he was a stunning pitcher. At other times he was just an ordinary pitcher. There is no rule that requires all talented players in baseball to love the game and be dedicated to it, and perhaps McDowell was one who would someday find more satisfaction in another field.

Samuel Edward McDowell was born September 21st, 1942, in Pittsburgh, and made his off-season home in the Pittsburgh suburb of Monroeville. His father, Thomas, a steel-mill inspector, was a former subsitute quarterback at the University of Pittsburgh. He was devoted to sports and eager for his son to succeed in sports.

Sam had five brothers and a sister. A grandfather and an uncle also lived with them in a four-bedroom home. There were few luxuries. Sam was the most talented athlete in the family and soon became his father's brightest hope. Sam began his athletic career as an eight-year-old outfielder on a team managed by his dad. Every player on the team was older than Sam.

"Ever since I can remember, my dad always played me with kids older than I was," Sam has said. "I can remember him saying it would make me better." One summer he played six times a week with three different teams. To play with one team he had to travel 32 miles by streetcar, hitch-hiking and walking.

But Sam longed to do other things. "One time I left the house with my streetclothes on under my uniform," he has recalled. "When I was out of sight, I took off my uniform and hid it and killed the day doing nothing. When it was time to come home, I put on my uniform and rubbed dirt on it so it looked like I'd been playing. But Dad found out."

Wistfully Sam said, "I never wanted to be a baseball player like most kids. I'd just as soon have been a teacher or something. I like the certainty of a 9-to-5 job. There's no certainty in baseball. But my father knew I had the talent, so he forced me into it."

His father demanded a great deal of his play. "My dad has never complimented me yet," Sam has said. "He'd always find something wrong. No matter what I did, he found a way that I could do better. No matter how many awards and prizes I got, I just wanted to please him more than anything else and since he would not let himself be pleased, I could not let myself be, either."

Sam recalled, "I pitched my first no-hitter for the Morningside Bulldogs. They gave a quart of ice cream for such accomplishments. I was dying for that ice cream, but dad said, 'The heck with it, let's go home.' Mom sneaked it out to me."

Sam grew up unsure of himself. "I had no confidence. I used to go out there hoping just not to embarrass myself instead of trying to win big." Years later he felt the same way: "No matter what I do, it never seems to be enough. Perhaps I am not as gifted as everyone thinks."

Yet in high school he was outstanding at baseball, basketball and football. He wanted to go to college and become a quarterback, but his father insisted he stick to baseball. In his senior year at Central Catholic High School Sam won eight of nine decisions, struck out 152 batters in 63 innings and did not permit a single earned run. Every team in the major leagues sought to sign him.

He had lived four blocks from Forbes Field, the home of the Pittsburgh Pirates, and had been invited to pitch batting practice for them on and off for two seasons. But McDowell finally signed with the Cleveland Indians for a $75,000 bonus. "I wanted to sign with the Pirates because it was my home-town team, but they didn't want to give me much of a bonus," he recalls.

With his early bonus money he bought his family a 15-room house. While he thought his father had pushed him into baseball, he also thought his father did what he felt was right for his son. "I love my father," he once said. "I always knew my father loved me. He took time for me. He just wanted me to make the most of my God-given talents."

Starting his professional career at 17, Sam was scared. In those early years he was so nervous before games his stomach muscles would tighten up and he'd feel sick. Even years later he said, "I just don't believe in being confident. I'm scared of losing. I worry. I worry sometimes that I'm not worried enough. I pitch best out of fear."

He started at Lakeland, Florida, in the Florida State League the last half of the 1960 season, winning five games and losing six. In 1961 he was moved all the way up to Salt Lake City of the Pacific Coast League, where he compiled a 13-10 record despite an awful 4.42 earned run average. He led the league in strikeouts with 156, but also in walks with 152. At season's end he appeared in one game for Cleveland and pitched six shutout innings.

Then and in the years to follow he was hailed as "the new Bob Feller" or "the new Sandy Koufax," the new super-pitcher of the major leagues. This put tremendous pressure on him and he was not equal to it.

McDowell opened the 1962 season in Cleveland. He won three and lost seven, was hit hard and was sent back to Salt Lake City in the minors. There he won three of five decisions. He opened the 1963 season with Cleveland, won three of eight decisions, was hit hard and was again sent down, this time to Jacksonville, Florida, of the International League. Here he won three of nine decisions.

In these early days Sam only knew how to throw his fast ball and his control was bad. After walking men on, he would get careful, slow down the fast ball and get hit. Then he would go back to firing. "I got speed crazy," he admits. "One of my minor league managers asked for more speed when I wasn't throwing quite as hard and had fair control. So I began to rare back and throw with all my might, gaining speed and losing control. I was pretty mixed up." He also developed a sore arm.

After spring training in 1964 Cleveland general manager Gabe Paul called McDowell in and scolded him for wasting his talent. He told Sam that he was being sent down again, this time to Portland of the Pacific Coast League. McDowell begged for a week to straighten himself out but was refused. "Paul said some things that made me boil," McDowell later recalled, "but I realize now he did it intentionally and it was just the thing I needed. The only thing I wanted to do was prove he was wrong, which is exactly how he wanted me to feel."

However, first Sam tried to quit. "Here I was, a failure at 20. I was beginning to wonder if it might not be better for me to get out while I was still young enough to go back to school." He wrote a letter to Gabe Paul announcing his resignation, apologizing for his performance and offering to return the balance of his bonus money. He showed the letter to

Portland manager Johnny Lipon, who advised him to hold it for awhile and to give it one more good try first. Sam agreed.

He won eight straight games, including a no-hitter against his old Salt Lake City team and two one-hitters. He struck out 102 batters in 76 innings. The Indians hurriedly summoned him back to Cleveland, where he achieved an 11-6 record with 177 strikeouts in 171 innings and a 2.71 ERA. It seemed Sam had arrived. He ripped up his letter of resignation. Yankee pitcher Whitey Ford said, "It is not possible to throw any faster than McDowell does." Cleveland manager Al Dark said, "He could be better than Koufax."

It was not that easy. The next year, 1965, he won 17 and lost 11. He led the league in strikeouts with 325, the third best record in major league history, and in earned run average with an excellent 2.18. But the following season he slipped to a 9-8 record and the season after that, saddled with another sore arm, he went 13-15 with a horrible 3.85 ERA. In 1968 he bounced back to 15-14 with a 1.81 ERA, and the next year he was 18-14 with a 2.94 ERA. Four times he had led the league in strikeouts, but three times he led in walks allowed in a season and twice in wild pitches.

McDowell developed a dazzling curve and sinker and at his best, he was awesome. Early in 1966 he set a major league mark by pitching two consecutive one-hitters. By the end of the 1960s he had tossed seven one-hitters, though he still was looking for his first no-hitter in the majors. He also set American League records by once striking out 30 men in two consecutive games and twice striking out 40 in three consecutive games. By the end of the 1960s he had 1,663 strikeouts in 1,589 innings. He and Sandy Koufax were the only pitchers ever to average better than a strikeout an inning.

Most pitchers begin to warm up before games by tossing the ball softly to the catcher from 40 feet away. Gradually they work their way back to the pitcher's distance of 60 feet, 6 inches and build up their speed. McDowell started from 80 feet and threw hard right away, his ball blazing and thundering into the catcher's mitt. Instead of gently breaking off his first curves, he snapped them off. Rivals watched him in awe.

Around baseball McDowell generally was regarded as having the fastest ball and best stuff in the game. Alvin Dark said, "If he could only relax, he could be as great as anyone ever was." But he couldn't relax and he couldn't seem to concentrate all the time. "I don't have the gift of concentration, so I have to keep reminding myself of things I have to do," Sam concedes. "I do it by talking to myself on the mound."

Dean Chance once said, "Sam McDowell is the best pitcher in the American League. He is overpowering. Anytime Sam is pitching, the game is a mismatch." McDowell replied, "That's nice of Dean to say that, but I haven't been involved in many mismatches yet."

In McDowell's defense, he received poor support from Cleveland. In 1968 he lost nine games by one run, two by 1-0 scores. In six of his games the Indians were shut out. But he often beat himself, often giving up a key hit in the clutch. Reggie Jackson has said, "I like facing McDowell. Not that he's not tremendous, but he gives you a challenge and a chance because he likes to match his strength against yours. He'll throw you the pitch you like to hit best and dare you to hit it. Any good hitter will take that dare."

McDowell liked to give batters that kind of challenge. "A game to me is a series of individual challenges—me against Reggie Jackson or me against Don Mincher," he said once. "If I find I can get a guy out with a fast ball, it takes all the challenge away so next time I throw him all curves. It makes the game more interesting."

A Cleveland broadcaster once said, "McDowell has a million-dollar arm and a ten-cent head." Frustrated by his failures and disappointed by his defeats, his critics have ridiculed him publicly more than once. Naturally this disturbed McDowell, but he learned slowly to take criticism in stride, as all top athletes must do. He had a lapse in 1970, however, when he had a verbal battle with a Cleveland announcer who had called McDowell a "national disgrace" when he had trouble winning his 19th game. Sam finally won the magic 20 and lost twelve.

McDowell has insisted, "I've matured. Nobody can force you or teach you to be mature, but, really, maturity is nothing more than concentration and the realization that God gives you some spectacular talents that should be put to proper use. Maturity is also the realization that other people—your family and friends, your teammates, even your fans, people you've never met—are relying on you and expect you to do your best."

Under the guidance of Cleveland pitching coaches Jack Sanford and Cotton Deal, Sam learned some of the science of his profession. "Before, all I ever was

McDowell blazes in a fast ball.

taught were the mechanics," he said. "But Sanford and Deal have begun to teach me the philosophy of pitching, the hows and whys of pitching. Pitching is not a guessing game. Now I'll give a good fast-ball hitter my fastball, but not where he's expecting it. I'm thinking now. My control is improved and I want to be a smart pitcher.

"I'd like to set all the strikeout records, naturally. Who wouldn't? I enjoy getting strikeouts and I know the fans enjoy seeing me get them. But I'd rather win games. If by throwing hard for a strikeout I'm risking giving up a critical hit, I won't do it. What good is it to strike out 15 or 16 batters and lose? Isn't it better to strike out five or six and win? I'd like to win the strikeout championship every year, but I'd rather win 20 games this year and next year and the year after that."

McDowell sported long hair and sideburns. He also entered games with a stubble of beard that made him seem menacing. "I never shave on days I pitch. It helps me feel mean," he said. He also refused to sign autographs or pose for pictures on days that he pitched.

Baseball legend says that left-hand pitchers are stranger than other souls and take a long time to find the right way. In 1970 Sudden Sam seemed to be giving some support to this myth.

He started fast, winning 13 games by midseason. Although he had to struggle in the second half, he finished at 20-12, struck out 304 batters in 305 innings and compiled a fine 2.92 earned run average.

It was the second time he had struck out 300 batters in a season and his career total was approaching the 2,000 mark.

Late in the year he received little help from his team and admitted that he was "very tired." But at season's end he was named Pitcher of the Year in the American League in a poll of players conducted by *The Sporting News*. Sam was pleased. He said, "The honor means especially much to me because it was voted by the other players. More than anything else, athletes want the respect of their peers."

Possibly the later seasons will show that McDowell was indeed the successor of Bob Feller and Sandy Koufax. He has said, "I want to be number one—number one in all of baseball. What's wrong with that? I think it's good to set goals and then strive for them."

Most important for McDowell is keeping up his interest in the challenges baseball has to offer. "The only thing I get satisfaction from is accomplishing something I'm not supposed to be able to do," he once said. "I live for challenges and once I overcome them, I have to go on to something new."

9. BOB GIBSON

IN THE SEVENTH GAME of the 1967 World Series at Fenway Park in Boston, Bob Gibson of the St. Louis Cardinals opposed Jim Lonborg of the Red Sox. Gibson had suffered a broken leg early in the season and had won only 13 games. Lonborg had won 22 games and the Cy Young award as the best pitcher in the American League. Lonborg and Gibson had each won two of the earlier World Series games. It was a classic match.

The hard-throwing Gibson walked the leadoff batter, but then retired the next 12 Red Sox in a row, striking out seven. Meanwhile, in the Cardinal half of the third inning, Dal Maxvill tripled off the wall in center. With two out Curt Flood singled in a run. Then Roger Maris singled and Lonborg allowed a second run to score on a wild pitch. The Boston fans groaned.

In the Cardinal fifth Gibson came to bat against his opponent and rocketed a 380-foot home run into the center-field bleachers. The Cardinals scored

Third baseman Mike Shannon (left), catcher Tim McCarver and first baseman Orlando Cepeda are the first to congratulate Gibson after he has defeated Boston in the 1967 World Series.

twice more in the inning and Gibson led, 5-0. The Red Sox scored once in the bottom of the fifth on a triple by George Scott and a Cardinal error.

In the sixth the Cardinals scored two more runs when Julian Javier hit a home run with a man on. Lonborg left the game and Gibson seemed a certain winner with a 7-1 lead. But it had been a trying season for him. He was worn out from working with little rest, and the Red Sox remained dangerous.

The Sox scored another run in the eighth when Gibson fired a wild pitch with a man on third. The score was 7-2. At the end of the inning Gibson sat back wearily in the St. Louis dugout, sweat streaming down his face. The Cardinals failed to score in the top of the ninth and the big Cardinal pitcher walked slowly to the mound once more.

The first batter, Carl Yastrzemski, singled. It was only the third hit of the game off Gibson. Bob shook his head angrily and returned to his task. Dangerous Ken Harrelson moved in. Gibson got him to hit the ball to the infield for a double play. Burly George Scott was up. Gibson, working for the last out of a long season, mustered a little extra energy and fired the ball past Scott. He struck him out and the Cardinals became World Champions.

Pandemonium broke out among the Cardinals as they mobbed the man who had pitched them to the championship. He had won three of the Cardinals' four victories in the Series. With the two games he had won for the Cardinals in the 1964 World Series, he had five Series victories in a row.

In the clubhouse the Cardinals behaved like boys, shouting and laughing and playing pranks as they celebrated their dramatic triumph. Television cameramen and sportswriters surrounded Gibson. He was named the Most Valuable Player of the Series, winning a new sports car from *Sport* magazine.

Gibson was then at the pinnacle of success. He had grown up in a poor black neighborhood; he had been branded as a pitcher who choked in the clutch; he had suffered serious illnesses and injuries. But now he had gained recognition as one of the great pitchers and pressure performers in baseball.

His father, a mill worker, died of pneumonia before Robert Gibson was born on November 9th, 1935. He was the seventh child of a poor family. They lived in a four-room wooden shack in Omaha, Nebraska. Bob slept on an Army cot. He was once bitten on the ear by a rat during the night.

Bob's mother worked as an laundress and cleaning woman to support her children. An older brother, Leroy, nicknamed "Josh" after the old star of the black baseball leagues, Josh Gibson, worked to help out and was like a father to Bob. "Leroy would give me a whack on the behind whenever I did anything wrong," Bob recalled.

A sickly boy, Bob suffered from rickets, hay fever, asthma, pneumonia and a rheumatic heart while growing up. He tried to be as tough as his pals, but it was difficult for him. Although he lived in a rough neighborhood, he avoided serious trouble. When he was seven, he broke into an old barn and took a keg which turned out to contain rusty nails. He was caught and he was arrested. He read comic books in a jail cell until his family bailed him out. This was his most serious crime.

Bob shined shoes in the downtown district of Omaha for badly needed money. What free time he had, he devoted to sports. "We played sports because we couldn't afford other things. There wasn't anything else to do except get in trouble," he recalled. Leroy worked at the YMCA, coached basketball and baseball, and gave Bob his first lessons.

Bob grew up late. The first time he went out for

his high school football team, he was rejected—he stood 4-foot-10 and weighed only 90 pounds. He was a day late for baseball tryouts and was not given another chance that year. He played for a YMCA team instead.

Eventually he became an outstanding baseball and basketball player and track performer in high school. At 15 he received a baseball offer from the Kansas City Monarchs, a prominent black team, but he was too young to take it. When he graduated from high school, he was disappointed to find he was not widely sought by college talent scouts. Through Leroy's influence he finally received a scholarship to Creighton University in Omaha. Here he continued his outstanding baseball and basketball play. But scouts for the pro teams seemed no more interested in him than college scouts had been.

Bob went to work at a service station from midnight to 7 a.m. every night to support himself. When the Harlem Globetrotters offered him a spot for $500 a month, he left school to tour with the basketball clowns for a season. Back home in Omaha he worked out with the local St. Louis Cardinal farm team. Johnny Keane, the manager of the Omaha team, offered him a $1,000 bonus to sign a contract. Bob accepted.

Gibson had been primarily an outfielder, but Keane felt Bob's future lay in pitching and he was a pitcher from then on. He divided the 1957 season, his first in pro baseball, between Omaha in the American Association and Columbus, Georgia, in the Sally League, winning six games and losing four. He divided the 1958 season between Omaha and Rochester, New York, in the International League, winning eight games and losing nine.

Gibson lacked mastery of sufficient stuff to win consistently, but the 6-foot-1, 195-pound right-hander could throw hard and he had good control. In 1959 he was 9-9 at Omaha. Late in the season he got his first chance with St. Louis. He won three and lost five. In 1960 he was 2-3 at Rochester and 3-6 at St. Louis.

He was going up and down between St. Louis and the minors like a yo-yo. He felt insecure and unsure of himself. "I didn't see a minor league game until I played in one, or a major league game until I played in one, not even on TV," he pointed out. He had no background in the business. And he was treated roughly by some of his bosses. Solly Hemus, the Cardinal manager in 1960, told him he'd never make a big league pitcher, Bob remembered, and the memory still angered him years later.

In 1961 Gibson opened with the Cardinals and had only a 2-6 record when Hemus was fired. The new manager was Johnny Keane, Bob's first professional manager. Bob went 11-6 the rest of the campaign. Gibson loved Keane, and Keane restored the young prospect's confidence in himself and polished him as a pitcher.

In 1962 Gibson compiled a 15-13 mark with 208 strikeouts and a 2.85 ERA. He missed the last week of the season when he caught his spikes in the dirt at

Pitching in the bottom of the tenth inning against the Yankees in the 1964 World Series, Gibson wins another game.

home plate during batting practice and broke a bone in his right ankle. In 1963 he went 18-9 with 204 strikeouts.

At this point in his career Gibson was 28 and an

established pitcher. But the word around the league was that if you were only a run or two behind him, you could beat him. When the pressure was on, it was said, Bob Gibson folded. Bob resented the suggestion that he was a "choker." He was also frustrated that he could not seem to move from his standing as a "good" pitcher and become a great one.

In 1964 Gibson was struggling with a 10-10 record on August 15th. The Cardinals were 9 1/2 games behind the league-leading Phillies. In the last six weeks of the season Gibson won nine of 11 decisions and the Cardinals won the pennant as the Phils collapsed. After that no one ever commented adversely about Gibson's performance under pressure.

Johnny Keane said, "He gave so much of himself on every pitch that he tired late in games. He had to learn to pace himself. But he had everything else for greatness." Gibson said, "When a man believes in you as Keane did in me, you feel you can do anything."

Gibson started the second game of the World Series against the Yankees and left the game with the Cardinals behind 2-1. The Cards eventually lost, 8-3.

With the Series tied at two games apiece, Gibson worked the fifth game in Yankee Stadium. He led the Yankees 2-0, going into the ninth. But an infield hit by Mickey Mantle and a home run by Tom Tresh tied the game. In the Cardinal half of the tenth Tim McCarver hit a three-run homer to put the Cards ahead 5-2. Gibson protected the lead in the last of the tenth and got credit for the win.

The Yankees won the sixth game. Keane called on Gibson to pitch the decisive seventh game with only two days' rest. The Cardinals surged to a 6-0 lead after five innings. Gibson, tiring in the late innings, gave up a three-run homer to Mantle in the sixth. He got through the seventh and eighth innings without allowing another Yankee run. In the meantime, the Cardinals' Ken Boyer hit a home run. Going into the last of the ninth, Gibson had 7-3 lead.

In the last of the ninth Tom Tresh struck out, but Clete Boyer hit a home run, making it 7-4. Then John Blanchard struck out, but Phil Linz hit a home run. It was 7-5 and the exhausted Gibson was struggling. Johnny Keane went to the mound to talk to his pitcher. "I want you to finish this," he said. Gibson nodded. "I was committed to his heart," Keane commented later.

Gibson bent in against Bobby Richardson, who had already collected 13 hits in the Series. Big Bob fired a fastball in tight and Richardson popped it up. Second baseman Dal Maxvill caught it and the Cardinals had their first world championship since 1946. Gibson, acclaimed the most valuable player of the classic, had compiled 31 strikeouts in 27 innings. Cheered in the clubhouse later, he admitted, "I feel like I've been in a gangfight and I was the only guy in my gang."

After the World Series Keane left the Cardinals to manage the Yankees. Red Schoendienst took over as skipper of the Cardinals in 1965 and they fell to seventh place. Still Gibson was solid, winning 20, losing 12 and striking out his all-time personal high of 270 batters. The following season the Cards settled for sixth place, but Gibson went 21-12 with 225 strikeouts.

In July of 1967 Gibson was pitching against Pittsburgh when a line drive hit by Roberto Clemente struck his right leg. Bob pitched to three more batters, retiring the side, before returning to the dugout. He was limping and in pain. So he was rushed to the hospital for an examination, which disclosed a broken bone. The break was set and placed in a cast.

The Cards were off to a fast start and fighting for first place. Gibson was impatient. Two weeks after his accident, he had his cast off and was telling Schoendienst he was ready to go. Schoendienst and the doctors asked him to be patient. Five weeks after the accident Gibson resumed working out and three weeks after that, in early September, he resumed pitching.

Gibson pitched five times in the last weeks of the season and the Cards captured the pennant. He entered the World Series still rusty with a mere 13-7 record. When he won three games against the Red Sox, he suddenly was the most celebrated athlete in sports.

Gibson took his laurels in stride. He was a sensitive and moody person who had unpleasant memories of growing up in the ghetto. He felt that had he not been black, he would have been sought with more determination by college and professional scouts. He remembered incidents of racial prejudice in baseball, especially in the minor leagues in the south. He was committed to the cause of civil rights. "A man must do his thing, no matter what it may be," he has said. "My thing is baseball. It is what I used to escape the ghetto and it is what I must use to make whatever contributions I can."

During the off-season Gibson lived quietly with his wife and family in Omaha, avoiding the glamour of other celebrities' lives. He had little patience with the press and considered publicity at best a necessary evil. He often was short with fans who hounded him when he appeared in public.

"Just say you were a garbage collector and every day about a hundred people stopped you and asked how much garbage you collected that day and how much you expected to collect the next day," he explained. "I would welcome someone who came up to me and wanted to talk to me as though I were a person and one who could talk about something besides last night's game or tomorrow's game." Concluded Gibson, "All I owe the fans is the best performances I can give them."

This much he certainly gave. He admitted that he pitched in pain almost constantly. "My arm always hurts," he once confessed. "I can't remember a time since 1963 when it hasn't hurt during a game or right after it. The human arm is not built to take the punishment of throwing 100 pitches a game every fourth or fifth day seven months a year for ten years." Yet, despite bone chips and arthritis in his right elbow, he worked his aching arm until it almost fell off, starting 30 to 40 games a season, pitching around 300 innings every season. "I've never come out of a game on my own," he has said. "I've never asked a manager to take me out. Never."

Glaring in at the batters, working with almost deadly determination, Gibson simply overpowered most of his foes. He had a scorching fast ball, a sharp curve and a tricky slider, and when his stuff was working, he was tremendous.

In 1968, shortly after Don Drysdale completed his record streak of six straight shutouts and 58 2/3 consecutive scoreless innings, Gibson almost matched him. Bob shut out five straight foes. Matched with Drysdale in Dodger Stadium as he sought a sixth straight, Gibson gave up a run in the first inning on two singles and a wild pitch. However, he then went on to win the game, 5-1. And he continued to stretch new strings of shutout innings until he had given up only three runs over 100 innings, which ranks as one of the most remarkable achievements in pitching history.

Bob won 15 straight at one point that season, wound up with a 22-9 record, a league-leading 268 strikeouts and an all-time National League record low earned-run average of 1.12, which he considered his greatest record. He completed the amazing total of 28 out of 34 starts. He led the league with 13 shutouts. He not only received the Cy Young award as the top pitcher, but was voted the Most Valuable

Player in the league, a rare distinction for a pitcher.

The Cardinals were carried by Bob to another pennant, which put him back under pressure as their "money pitcher" in the World Series. Facing Detroit in the first game, Gibson was incredible. Prior to that game Sandy Koufax had the record for strikeouts in a single World Series contest with 15. Gibson entered the ninth inning with 14 strikeouts and a 4-0 lead.

Mickey Stanley, the first Tiger up in the ninth, singled. Then Gibson struck out Kaline, Cash and Horton to set a new record of 17 strikeouts in a World Series game. Bob swears he was unaware of the record until after the sixteenth man had struck out and the game was held up while the fans cheered his accomplishment. He turned around and looked at the scoreboard. It said, "Sixteen strikeouts."

Three days later Gibson opposed Denny McLain, that season's celebrated 30-game winner, and slaughtered him, 10-1. He set a new World Series record by gaining his seventh straight complete-game victory. He also hit a home run, his second in World Series competition.

But Detroit was determined and battled back to tie the Series at three games apiece. In the seventh game Gibson returned to oppose Detroit's Mickey Lolich, who had already won two games. Arm-sore and weary, Gibson was wonderful, holding his foes to one hit, an infield single, through the first six innings. Lolich had a four-hitter to that point. Both sides were scoreless.

With two out in the seventh Detroit's Norm Cash lined a single. Horton bounced a single through the infield. Gibson bore down. Jim Northrup hit a fly ball deep to center. Centerfielder Curt Flood misjudged it. He started to come in for the ball, then started to run back. But he was too late and the ball fell free. It was scored as a triple and two runs scored. Freehan then hit the ball to left-center. Lou Brock reached for it, but it bounced in front of his glove and a third run scored.

Gibson stood quietly on the mound, seemingly expressionless, his streak shattered, but his courage and composure solid. He struck out Don Wert to end the inning. And he finished the game, giving up another run in the ninth. Lolich gave up one run in the ninth, too, but the Tigers had won, 4-1. Gibson walked quietly off the mound, ignoring the celebration of the Tigers. He remained as imposing a figure as ever.

In 1969 the Cardinals dropped from contention, but Gibson completed the decade as one of the dominant pitchers of that period with a 20-13 record, 269 strikeouts and a 2.18 ERA. And in 1970 he came back with another superb season.

He completed 23 of 34 starts, worked 294 innings, and struck out 274 batters. He had a 23-7 record and a fine 3.12 earned run average. It was the eighth season in which he had struck out 200 batters, a major league record. He needed only ten more wins to reach the 200 mark and passed Sandy Koufax in the career strikeouts list, with 2,413.

In a good mood, Gibson does calisthenics to get in shape for another season.

Although Gibson started slowly in 1970, he finished with a flourish. At 35 he was still a powerful pitcher—perhaps the best in the league. At the end of the season he was awarded the Cy Young award in recognition of his great year. And he still had many milestones within reach—his 200th win, his 2,500th strikeout and perhaps another amazing World Series performance.

By 1970 Johnny Keane, who gave Gibson his first chance, had died. But before he passed on, he paid Gibson perhaps his ultimate compliment. He said,

"There have been many pitching stars in recent years. But none has shone brighter than Bob Gibson. Perhaps some have excelled him in the regular season, though that isn't clear. But the ultimate in baseball is the World Series. Not all pitchers get to face this test very often. But it is the true test. And Bob Gibson had to face that awful pressure more than most and passed through it better than any. When you are talking of major league professional pitchers of recent years, he has been the truest."

INDEX

Page numbers in italics refer to photographs

EXTRA DRY
Lager Beer

NATIONAL
R P IG
CHI 1 6
PIT 1 8
LA 1 3
C!N 1 9
HOU 3 2
MIL 2 8
SF 2 10
STL 2 7
METS
9 CF
33 2B
21 1B
23 RF
12 C
19 LF
1 SS
2
49
H-E
AT BAT 49
BALL 2
1 2 3 4 5 6
PHILA. 1 1 0 0 0 4
N Y METS 0 0 0 0 0 0
TOP BRASS
MEDICATED HAIR DRESSING
Let's go METS!
as good to your taste
Rheingol

96